BREXIT
A Remainer's Guide to Brexiteers

Keith McGivern

Copyright © 2019 Keith McGivern

All rights reserved.

ISBN:
ISBN-9781798879771

DEDICATION

I dedicate this book to my wife Claire and my son Eóin, without whom I would never have been inspired enough to write.

I love you both more than anything in the world and hope for your sake that what is outlined in this book never comes to pass

CONTENTS

	The Foreword	Pg 1
	Part One – The Cause	Pg 7
1	The Referendum	Pg 7
2	The Average man in the street	Pg 11
3	The 350 Million brigade	Pg 15
4	The Eurosceptic	Pg 19
5	The Have your cake and eat it crowd	Pg 24
6	The Protest vote	Pg 29
7	The Over 65s	Pg 32
8	The Xenephobe	Pg 39
9	The String pullers and those who seek to gain	Pg 43

Part Two – The Effect   Pg 46

10   The Unsuspecting European union citizen building a life in the UK   Pg 46

11   The Backstop and the elephant in the room, Ireland   Pg 50

12   The NHS   Pg 59

13   The Farming industry   Pg 67

14   The Bankers and big business   Pg 71

15   The Scientific and research community   Pg 83

16   The Lorry car park in Kent   Pg 87

17   The Politics   Pg 93

     The Conclusion   Pg 107

     Afterword   Pg 123

THE FOREWORD

31st of January 2019: 57 days until the UK is due to leave the European Union…

… and the day I decided to write this book.

1: I've heard countless times over the past two and a half years how in years to come people will write books about Brexit and its role in the economic self-harm/suicide of a nation.

2: I've heard from many individuals, both friend and foe, how nothing we do as individuals really matters and how we can't effect change in any substantial way.

3: Being from Northern Ireland, with our relatively small population, I've heard that even if every person within Northern Ireland voted to Remain in the referendum on the 23rd of June 2016, collectively as a nation the United Kingdom would still have voted to leave overall.

I have little doubt that the first of those points will come to pass, regardless of whether we do eventually leave the European Union with or without a deal.

The last of those three points is factually correct, and elaborated upon later in this book.

The second of those points however I wholeheartedly believe is not true.

May/June 2016:

Growing up in Northern Ireland in the 1980s and 1990s politics was always present in the background, although I was never particularly interested in it. My family, thankfully were never particularly politically motivated, nor were the majority of my friends. Many in Northern Ireland back then and today were and are extremely politically motivated, that's entirely justifiable given Northern Ireland's troubled history. I was lucky in that my immediate family had never experienced hardship as a result of the troubles. The IRA planted a bomb in the pub in Distillery street, where my Granny and Grandad used to live, and it damaged their house, meaning they had to move out. But compared to many in Northern Ireland we got off extremely lightly. People's fathers, sons, mothers and daughters were killed simply because of their religion in what was effectively a tit for tat civil war. Catholics were murdered on Friday night and Protestants were murdered the following Monday. There might have been a week or two week break then it happened again but this went on for many years and many hundreds of families and thousands of individuals lives were destroyed. This is not a situation I believe many in Northern Ireland want to return to. Yet I fear that in the event of a hard border being put in place between the North and the South of Ireland that may well be what we are heading towards with the potential collapse of the Good Friday Agreement. Various politicians in the Conservative party have stated recently that there was never a hard border in Ireland, that it was fantasy. As someone who actually lived in Northern Ireland and travelled across that border many times, it certainly did exist. Not only did it exist but it was manned by British Soldiers with machine guns and was often an intimidating barrier to cross even as a child. I for one do not want my child to ever have to experience that in his lifetime.

Prior to April or May 2016 I had extremely limited exposure to politics directly. That's still the case but over the past two and a half years I've digested a lot of information from a plethora of sources and tried to educate myself on the subject. The main motivation to inform myself was because, with the Brexit Referendum, a decision that was essentially out of my hands stood to potentially impact myself and my family in a variety of ways. Hence, I decided that it was important to read up as much as I could on the subject, in an attempt to come to a well informed decision having taken an unbiased view on the pros and cons.

I came to the decision that, in my opinion it was in the UK's best interests to remain a part of the European Union. I'll not go into the reasons for that decision right now but suffice to say that come June 2016 my views were quite strong on the topic. I spoke to many friends and family on the subject of the referendum and was largely met with apathy. Few people in my immediate circle had read up much on Brexit and what it might mean. Some were planning on voting to Remain, some to leave, many were undecided. I took it upon myself to try to bring those who had decided they wanted to leave round to my way of thinking, that the decision to Remain was the better option. In the run up to the referendum I convinced both family and several friends who were intending on voting to leave the European Union that collectively we would be better off Remaining. Those few individuals who actually changed their vote based on my arguments prove that individuals can make a difference.

The purpose of this book and its timing came about because I decided one afternoon on a short lunchtime trip home from work, whilst listening to yet more endless Brexit debate on the news - that one man can indeed make a difference. This short book is just my opinion backed up with some references and facts from various sources about the impact Brexit and the vote to leave has had thus far on society as a whole and how leaving the European union with or without a deal might impact a number of key aspects of everyday life going forward. It contains my opinions on why the UK voted to leave back in 2016 and why I think it's important that Remainers and Brexiteers alike try to respectfully consider other people's views. Why they are entitled to those views and to try to help people realise that the other side isn't all evil or stupid as I seem to hear on an ever increasing basis as we approach March 29th 2019. People had their reasons why they voted the way they did, as they are entitled to in a democracy.

I want to try to put myself in the shoes of a Brexiteer, understand some of the things that helped to motivate a typical Leave voter in 2016 and if in doing so I can help to get across some of the viewpoints held by myself, as a Remain voter then I may just succeed in making that small difference. If at the same time I can try to help other Remain voters realise that they too can make a difference and that most people who voted to Leave did not do so for silly or selfish reasons, many of them did so because from their perspective it was the correct decision to make at the time, then I think collectively we have a much better chance of making a larger difference.

Leave Voter Read This Paragraph:
During the referendum you voted to Leave because you thought it was the correct decision to make, since the

referendum you've grown sick and tired of hearing endless project fear ad infinitum. You've grown tired of being called stupid or racist or too old for it to matter to you or countless other narrow minded comments from self righteous Remain voters who have their ideas about Brexit, about how and why you voted the way you did and they are unwilling to listen to your opinions about why you voted the way you did.

Remain Voter Read This Paragraph:
During the referendum you tried convincing Leave voters about the error of their ways. You've spent time trying to convince people who just won't listen, you've wanted to say I told you so countless times but have held your tongue on more than one occasion. You've tutted and shrugged, rolled your eyes as you listened to a Leave voter repeat the debunked facts that were spouted by the Leave campaign before during and after the referendum. You now worry about the very real possibility of a no deal Brexit and the social, economic and political disaster that would ensue, and in the case of Northern Ireland you worry about the very real possibility of a gradual return to the conflict that we all hoped we had escaped forever.

Non Voter Read This Paragraph:
You didn't vote last time around because you weren't sure how to vote, it was raining (Londoners I'm looking at you), you didn't think it would impact you or you weren't sure how it would impact you. You were literally lost amongst the sheer volume of information and opinions out there and didn't feel well informed enough to vote or you simply didn't care enough to vote. If you fall into that last category then my question to you is why? If you work you'll be impacted, if you don't work you'll be impacted, if you have children or plan to in the future they will be impacted and in my opinion it's almost a moral obligation to cast a vote when the

decision can and will impact all of our lives in a much more profound way than many people realise.

Part One – The Cause

1
THE REFERENDUM

On Christmas Day 2015 my wife and I got engaged. She claims she only said yes because I went down on two knees as opposed to one. We then went to Paris for a few days and on our return we booked the first venue we visited for our wedding. The date was set as the 10th of December 2016, not an awfully long time to plan and save for a wedding. We chose a hotel in Donegal which turned out to be a fantastic venue and is still our favourite hotel in Ireland and in fact anywhere we've been. One thing we certainly hadn't considered in January 2016 when booking a venue in the South of Ireland was the upcoming Brexit referendum. The referendum had not been announced at that stage and whilst David Cameron had promised a referendum in 2013 it wasn't exactly on our radar. On the 20th of February 2016 the referendum was announced and the date set as the 23rd of June 2016. Over the coming weeks I started to pay attention.

A couple of years earlier I had worked in the IT division of an Investment Bank in Belfast. We looked after the IT systems being used for various banking departments at the bank's European headquarters in London. Lots of big global banks have their European headquarters in London. Almost everybody was exposed in some way or another to the financial crisis that began to take root across the globe in 2007 and 2008 so we all remember it, many economies still haven't fully recovered. We all know that investment banks took the brunt of the blame for that collective calamity, the 2016 film entitled "The Big Short" does a brilliant job of explaining what happened to anyone who's not familiar. Not all banks and not all bankers were responsible but those that were managed to effectively crash the global economy in one fell swoop. The ongoing impact of that crisis can still be seen today across Britain and in fact the world as a whole. austerity has become a word synonymous with hardship for many families across the globe. In the UK the government systematically cut expenditure across swathes of departments to the point that food banks are now the norm for many working families.

During my time working for the investment bank I was exposed to lots of different business areas and various types of trading. I got to see how those systems worked and although we were never involved from the business perspective, within the IT departments we still developed a reasonable understanding of how financial markets worked from the inside. We got limited exposure to some of the high level decision making that helps to shape individual firms and the economy as a whole on national, continental and global scales.

Back in March 2016 with my rudimentary understanding of financial markets, gained whilst working for an investment bank I knew one thing for certain. That in the event of a Leave vote in the EU referendum sterling would take a severe hit against both the dollar and the Euro overnight. The initial reason why I decided to vote to Remain was therefore an entirely selfish one. With myself and my wife working in Northern Ireland (and therefore being paid in Sterling) but getting married in the South of Ireland (and therefore paying for the wedding largely in Euro) we would end up with a significantly heftier bill in the event of a Leave vote.

Over the course of the next few months into April, May and June 2016 I read more and more about the economy, about the European Union, immigration and about the likely consequences of a vote to Leave vs a vote to Remain. I watched countless videos, and read opinion pieces from 'experts'. The more I learned the more strongly I felt that the decision to Remain was the correct one. I started to share things on social media, it got to the point where some people likely blocked me. I had more and more discussions with people on the referendum and what way they were leaning so people probably avoided me in person as well. At this stage we are all sick of hearing about Brexit but for my friends and family that point was likely crossed back in June 2016.

To say I felt strongly is an understatement, the day after the result I posted a rant on social media that was epic in length if not necessarily in content. I got quite a lot of likes and shares, so much so that later that morning I was getting bombarded with abuse from Leave voters on shares of my post. It got to the point were I had to go to work so I removed the post rather than not be able to defend myself because I was otherwise engaged. The next day I tried again, I'd had time to cool down so I hope I was a bit more balanced in my approach.

From that initial selfish decision I made that I wanted to

Remain in February or March 2016 to the day of the result and my furious outburst. I'd metamorphosed from someone who cared little for politics to someone who was passionately engaged on the subject. I felt fully justified in the strength with which I would project my viewpoint because the more I learned the more I realised what a bad decision leaving was going to be for the country as a whole, not just me as an individual. Since then I believe I have cooled further, I would like to think that I'm now able to better consider the viewpoints of others and to realise that despite the decision to Leave or Remain being a binary black or white decision, people's reasons for voting the way they did were by no means binary. I now believe that everyone voted for their own reasons, whatever way they voted. Some reasons are more justified than others but each vote was equal and as a result I believe that the vote had to be respected with a legitimate *attempt* to Leave the European Union. I'll come back to that point later on but for now I'm going to move on to some of the motivations I believe played a major part in the mindsets of many typical Leave voters. Not every Leave voter will recognise the groups I outline in the following chapters but no list such as this could ever hope to be complete. I do however believe that a large number of those who voted to Leave will in fact recognise a number of the motivations I outline and believe that they belong in one or more of these groupings.

2
THE AVERAGE MAN IN THE STREET

In the last chapter I outlined some of the reasons why I came to the conclusions I came to in 2016 and why I personally felt that the best decision for myself as an individual and for the UK as a whole was to Remain.

Two people can have the same information but interpret it in completely different ways. People differ in how they value things, their hopes, fears and insecurities are all unique. Some people judge a situation in one way whilst others judge it differently, these are the simple facts of human nature. The same is true in politics, we all vote in different ways for vastly differing reasons. Some vote on instinct, some because it's the way they've always voted. Some vote because their family have a certain voting tradition, others vote based on the information they obtain and some people vote purely based on sound bytes and media opinion. I voted to Remain in the 2016 referendum because I had weighed up the options and made up my mind based on the information I had. I admitted in the previous chapter that my initial reasons were based on short term personal financial gain. However by the time the 23rd of June came around I believe that the reasons I voted to Remain were more balanced, justified and more long term in terms of foresight. I believe many people who voted to Leave did so for the same underlying reason, in that they truly believed it was the best decision for them personally and/or for the country as a whole.

Just some of the reasons I can see why people 'might' have voted to Leave included things like hospital and GP waiting lists - immigration has undoubtedly increased the UK population, not just immigration from the EU but immigration from across the globe. The UK has for many years been an aspirational country, like many other western European countries the UK's collective wealth and rich industrial history have made it an attractive place for many people from many countries. The same is true of other rich developed nations such as the United States, Canada and Australia. Leaving the EU may (or may not depending on the eventual deal, if there is a deal) stop freedom of movement from the EU, however one thing it certainly will not do is halt immigration. The main difference would likely be that some form of screening process will help to decide whom is or isn't allowed to enter the country. I'll discuss both the NHS and my views on immigration in a bit more detail in later chapters however I just wanted to touch on those points at this juncture.

Similar to hospital and GP waiting lists, I'm aware that many people voted to Leave due to things like school catchment areas and/or over subscription. Children who may or may not have been born in the UK will likely in some cases have been given school places ahead of children whose families have lived here for many generations. Those 'foreign' children won't have been given priority, they will simply have been lucky in that statistically they have as much chance of getting into a particular school as the next child. They have a right to an education and I don't believe that many right minded people would think otherwise. However, I can see a case where an individual might have seen things differently and blamed immigration on the fact that their child did not get into the school of their choice. In years to come presented with the same situation I myself may come to similar conclusions.

Chronic underfunding of public services under the government's austerity program has simply meant that the NHS can't deal with as many people as it needs to. Similarly there aren't enough teachers because teachers have effectively had to deal with real terms pay cuts (when inflation is factored in) over the last number of years. Schools aren't being given the budgets they need, teachers having no effective pay rises for ten years. As a result of these budget cuts schools simply aren't able to take in as many students as they potentially could with proper funding. Neither of those things is an immigrant from the EU, or any other country for that matters fault but it is still easy to see why people would let personal circumstance in relation to those areas help influence their opinions on the referendum. It's human nature.

The root then of both examples above is not the EU, rather it's aggressive budget cuts and austerity under the last nine years of Conservative government. The media had its part to play in pushing the message which came from our government on austerity. Suggesting that the country's finances were just like those of a household, in times of financial difficulty the most prudent course of action is to cut costs. This despite the fact that first year economics students know this is simply not the case and that a much more prosperous approach would have been to stimulate the economy with increased investment to promote growth. The media however were tasked with selling the public the lie that austerity was the only way forward. As a result we are now entering our ninth year of austerity despite the government's statement to the contrary that it is ending.

I am sure that there are many other relevant and valid reasons why perfectly rational and right minded people voted to Leave, but there are likely too many such reasons to list here. I simply wanted to make reference to the motivations listed above because I'm quite sure that a large number of people who voted Leave during the referendum did so for these and other valid reasons. The unfortunate truth however in relation to those particular two examples is that the decision to leave the EU, and consequently the reduced Gross Domestic Product (GDP) as a result, will almost certainly exacerbate such scenarios in the future if we leave the EU with a deal. If we leave without a deal then the government will be so financially crippled over the next few years that the austerity driven policies in the UK since 2010 will likely be dwarfed to such an extent that the NHS may exist in name only and education will only continue to be stretched to breaking point by ever decreasing budgets. Policing, the armed forces and practically every other governmental department will simply not have the funding they require to operate at current levels. We will all suffer as a result.

3
THE 350 MILLION BRIGADE

More has been said and written on this particular topic than any one individual could read in a lifetime. The simple fact of the matter is that many people did vote to Leave because they genuinely believed that if we left the EU then the NHS would be given an extra £350,000,000 per week. I deliberately put all of those zeros in there for impact, this is a huge number. Unfortunately it's an incorrect number in that literally as soon as we hand over £350,000,000 to the EU, every week, exactly half of that figure is given straight back. This as most people will be aware is due to the "Thatcher Rebate". For those who don't know what that is, the UK negotiated a rebate in 1984 which still stands to this day. It was negotiated to, in effect balance out the net contributions made by the UK because at the time the majority of the EU budget was spent on agricultural policy, and due to the way the UK farming sector was structured at the time the UK was one of the largest Net contributors to the EU but didn't get as much back in terms of funding as they might have expected. Other member states have also negotiated temporary reductions to their EU contributions, but the UK is in fact the only member who have a permanent reduction. People don't tend to read the details on topics such as this, it's a dry subject, you have to be interested (or extremely bored) and take the time to do a bit of research. The easiest thing to do is to simply look at the overall net contributions of the EU and quickly see that the UK sits third on the list, behind Germany and France, just ahead of Italy in fourth place. An even easier thing to do is take a number on the side of a big red bus and take it as fact despite a quick google search proving it to be a falsehood.

EU contributions are determined based on a number of factors including Gross National Income (GNI), a percentage of VAT receipts and customs duties on imports from outside the EU. Back in 1984 when it was negotiated, the Thatcher rebate was widely believed to be justified when looked at in the context of overall contributions vs EU funding in return. Today however when the figures are dissected the UK's rebate is much more difficult to justify. The UK in fact pays a lower percentage of its Gross National Income into the EU budget than any other nation in the EU, and by a considerable margin. At roughly 0.7% of GNI the UK pays less as a percentage than France (0.8%) Germany (0.9%), Ireland, Romania and Poland (1.0%), Slovenia (1.1%), Bulgaria and Latvia (1.2%) and finally Holland and Belgium who pay the most as a percentage of GNI at 1.3%.

Really at the minute we have quite a '***good deal***'.

The reason for this is that the rebate was negotiated in 1984 and implemented in 1985. Whist we are still members it won't be removed but were we to leave and subsequently rejoin the EU at a later date there would be no such rebate. The reasons why the rebate made sense in 1984 but doesn't today is because its thirty five years later - things change, industries change, economies change, new members have joined and all the while the UK's current deal has become more and more valuable over time. Other countries effectively have to subsidise Britain (France and Italy being the two most unfortunately burdened nations, paying more than they otherwise should to make up the UK shortfall due to the rebate).

I have personally heard from people who voted to leave simply because they believed that the impossible figure, the £350 million (which could only ever possibly have been £175 million) was definitely going to go straight to the NHS as soon as we left the European Union. This was never and could never have been the case yet leading Leave campaigners repeated it day after day for months on end as if it was fact. If I had voted to Leave based on that fantasy figure and a big red bus, then heard one of those same leading Leave campaigners deny it the day after the referendum i'm not sure how I would have reacted. To say I would have been unhappy might be a bit of an understatement, yet this actually happened to many people. Whether it was the official Vote Leave campaign or the Leave.EU campaign who commissioned that big red bus and the adverts which accompanied it matters little. The simple fact of the matter is that many hundreds of thousands of people, perhaps millions (though that seems difficult to believe) voted to Leave because they took that blatant bare faced lie to be fact. To me this literally beggars belief, to see it unfold and be denied on national television on the morning of 24th of June 2016, before fake news was literally all over the news, was hard to believe. Yet there it was, the smugness that accompanied that denial simply made it all the more difficult to watch.

The simple fact of the matter is that the NHS has been chronically underfunded for years now, its at crisis point in many towns and cities across the country. This is not in any way shape or form the fault of the EU, or the fault of EU nationals living in the UK. I hate to go back to the word that we have all heard far too many times over the past nine years but it all comes down to austerity, and austerity was the brainchild of Westminster not Brussels.

0.7% of GNI, that rather large figure at the start of this chapter £350,000,000 (or even the correct figure at £175,000,000) doesn't seem quite as big when you consider just how much money the government has to spend in total.

I don't pretend to be an economist, nor have I ever studied the subject in great depth but when 'experts' are all convinced that the UK's economy will suffer as a result of Brexit I tend to believe them. A little bit of independent research strongly supports their findings. Nobody has a crystal ball, nobody can predict the future with absolute certainty but we can be relatively certain that the UK as a whole will be worse off after Brexit, the only thing in dispute is the degree to which the economy stagnates or contracts. The NHS can only be worse off in such a scenario, one thing every single one of us can however be absolutely 100% certain of, is that after Brexit the NHS absolutely will not get an extra £350,000,000 per week, because it never really existed in the first place.

4
THE EUROSCEPTIC

Lots of people just don't like the European Union, not just in the UK but in other EU countries and further afield. The US president has called the EU a foe, Russia views the EU as a foe, the former on trade, the latter due to paranoia and underlying resentment, as well as a deep rooted fear that many former eastern bloc nations are integrating more fully and moving further toward the west. Many individuals also have a strong dislike of the EU and what it stands for. In Britain and across many European nations far right extremists are growing in influence. Those on the far right however are still thankfully in the minority, within mainstream society many view the EU as too bureaucratic, on the left many are disillusioned by EU rules around state aid. Parties with more socialist ideals can feel that their hands are somewhat tied by the inability to offer state aid to firms in what they may see as in the national interest. The reason such rules exist within the EU are due to the fact that within the single market, companies and individual nations could gain competitive advantage through state funding, they could therefore undercut the competition which goes against the principles of the common market.

One of the arguments which was widely marketed by the Leave campaign during the referendum was around the concept of sovereignty, taking back control of our laws etc. There is some truth to this in that the European Court of Justice trumps UK courts in terms of jurisdiction. There are rules such as those around state aid mentioned above. Rules around the safety of children's toys being imported into the EU, rules on environmental controls, on food safety on workers rights and many others which help to underpin how the EU works as a trading bloc. Those are there for a reason and they help to ensure that it functions as it's designed to.

Like any debate there are two sides to any argument, one of the ways the public was led to believe they were taking back sovereignty was by wresting control from those unelected bureaucrats in Brussels. This however happens to be yet another easily debunked Leave campaign myth. The UK currently has seventy three Members of the European Parliament. Those MEPs are there to act on the UK's behalf and look out for UK interests within the EU. The fact that UK turnout tends to be particularly low every time European Elections come around is not the fault of the EU, it's simply due to the public's general apathy (at least until Brexit came along) as regards European Politics on the whole.

UKIP has a more significant part to play in Brussels than they do back in the UK. The fact that their sole purpose and entire modus operandi was and is to extricate the UK from the EU is somewhat ironic. The reason they are over represented in the European parliament is simply because one group of their core voters, i.e. the Eurosceptics, tend to care much more about the EU than the average British voter. Low turnout in EU elections therefore favours these extreme parties and as such they end up with more power than they would have under any other circumstance.

Another theme running through Euroscepticism in Britain has been the reluctance to adopt the Euro. In fact that is not only an opinion held by Eurosceptics, but by the majority of the British population as a whole, ever increasingly over the last twenty or so years and particularly in light of the Greek economic crisis with the subsequent pressure that placed on the Eurozone.

Many who promote Euroscepticism however, tend to purport a myth that if we were to stay in the EU we would have had to adopt the Euro. The simple fact of the matter is that in during the negotiations of the Maastricht treaty in 1992 the UK government secured an opt out from the Euro, effectively allowing the UK to retain Sterling until the UK itself decided it no longer wanted to. Various opinion polls have been carried out over the years within the UK but never has support for adopting the Euro risen above the 33% support it received in June 2003. By 2012 support for adopting the Euro within the UK had fallen to a mere 6%, those figures were simply opinion polls and do not necessarily indicate what the figures might have been in the event of a referendum on the issue. One thing however that is clear, is that the actual real prospect of the UK joining the Euro was very low in the run up to the Brexit referendum in 2016. Not so if you believed some of the lies being spouted by prominent Leave campaigners, twas ever thus.

One of the lines we've heard regurgitated endlessly over the past number of years has been in relation to "the bureaucrats in Brussels." The definition of a Bureaucrat is as follows:

"an official in a government department, in particular one perceived as being concerned with procedural correctness at the expense of people's needs."

This is not a statement I disagree with, the European union does in fact have lots of rules and procedures, some of those I agree with and some I don't. The European Union do tend to tack quite a lot of red tape onto their policies, but that's no less true of many individual governments and governing bodies the world over. Some red tape is to be expected to manage a continent wide Single Market & Customs Union, in my opinion it's a small price to pay for the benefits that accrue to the UK from having access to the Single Market and the Customs Union. One additional thing to consider is that following Brexit there will be a huge amount of red tape involved in any post Brexit trade deals. Red tape is a fact of life in international trade. Complaining about it isn't necessarily helpful as it completely misses the point.

Despite the fact that I agree with the statement that sometimes, in some policy areas the EU can be overly bureaucratic, that in no way makes me a Eurosceptic. I believe that the vast majority of the rules and regulations we've inherited as members of the EU are of benefit to me as an individual and Britain as a whole. Human rights, workers rights, animal rights and food safety are all policy areas were we in the UK currently defer to European law. The reason those in full time employment in the UK are entitled to twenty three paid holidays per year (plus in many cases bank holidays) is due to the

EU. In the United states for example many full time workers only get ten days leave per year, this is one particular area I believe our current government would be more than happy to 'relax' the law given half a chance. I for one hope they never do but its a very real possibility after we leave the EU. Many companies will still continue to offer such benefits but the most vulnerable in society likely won't have that luxury. Similarly things like animal rights and food safety are currently governed by EU regulations. Our farmers have spent the past forty years bringing standards up to a point whereby British and Irish beef are now literally a label of quality the world over. Do we really want to roll that back and have our farmers try to compete with chlorine washed chicken or hormone enhanced beef from the United states? One of the often repeated myths during the referendum campaign was in relation to the EU regulations on bent bananas. The Leave campaign incorrectly stated that the EU dictated that bananas had to be straight rather than curved. That's simply not the case, in effect its a lie, the EU actually offers guidelines ensuring that bananas are classed based on their curvature and deformity, or lack thereof, with class A bananas being straighter and more pristine than their class B or C counterparts. Do we really care how bent our bananas are anyway? Why does it matter that bananas in our supermarkets tend to be straighter than they otherwise might be or are we simply cutting off our nose to spite our face?

5
THE HAVE YOUR CAKE AND EAT IT CROWD

Brexit has been a lesson in revisionism. Many things have been said over the past number of years only to be entirely contradicted hours, days, weeks or months later.

Leading Leave campaigners said that making a deal with the EU was going to be "the easiest deal in history", later to revise that to "we are not preparing for no deal because there is definitely going to be a deal", now that seems to have metamorphosed again into "there is no problem with no deal, that's what people voted for".

During the referendum campaign we were led to believe that we would continue to have access to the single market but wouldn't have to accept freedom of movement, oh and we wouldn't have to pay for it either. If the EU were to allow the UK such a deal then what would stop other EU countries demanding the same terms? It would literally break the EU's entire model. Quite why the party holding 95% of the bargaining chips in a negotiation would buckle to the unreasonable demands of the party holding 5% of the bargaining chips surely seems nonsensical. Yet these were the promises made by those who promoted the Leave campaign and subsequently lapped up by the masses.

We hear an awful lot about the Single Market and Customs union but the average citizen doesn't necessarily know what those terms actually mean in real terms and how they impact us in day to day life. When you are giving something up I think it's important to understand what it is you are giving up before taking that decision yet I'm sure a significant portion of Leave voters, and Remain voters alike for that matter do not fully understand the intricacies of those terms. I don't claim to fully understand them myself in every detail but I do have a rudimentary understanding which I've tried to outline below.

The Single Market consists of four freedoms, those freedoms are designed to increase competition, maintain high standards and help create a single trading bloc which has much more influence and leverage on a global scale than any of its constituent countries could ever hope to attain individually. The effect of this has historically helped give a boon to the member states individual economies and the success of the bloc as a whole. The single market guarantees the freedom of goods, capital, services and movement. Those four freedoms are tightly knit into British business and society as a whole offering many seen and unseen benefits.

Freedom of movement is a controversial topic for many within the UK and throughout Europe. It was certainly a major factor in the 2016 referendum. Freedom of movement and immigration as a whole however can have both positive and negative impacts, the most widely publicised of those unfortunately tend to have negative connotations. Within some sectors immigration may mean increased competition in terms of employment opportunities for British nationals, thats a simple fact and that fact could conceivably have had the effect of keeping wages within those sectors lower than they might otherwise have been. At an individual level, for people employed in those sectors it's easy to see why freedom of movement may have limited their employment and/or career prospects but many sectors simply would not function without freedom of movement. The NHS, farming and many other sectors would suffer immeasurably.

If the above statement is in fact true and some individuals earn less today than they otherwise might have done without freedom of movement then it's only fair that we examine the other side of that particular coin. Say for example you as a Leave voting individual working in an industry heavily staffed by EU citizens. For the purposes of this example let's assume you might earn 20% more today in 2019 without freedom of movement than you otherwise might have done with that freedom of movement. That would effectively make you earn an additional ten pounds for every fifty pounds that you currently do, not a bad situation taken at face value. Now consider that those sixty pounds in your pocket today are worth considerably less than sixty pounds would have been prior to the referendum, due to a combination of inflation and a significant drop in the value of sterling following the result.

Inflation today is running at a relatively smooth 2.5%, the Bank of England tries to maintain a target rate of inflation of 2%, the reason the government want a certain amount of inflation is due to the fact that moderate inflation helps the economy to grow. Historically however inflation rates have been much higher, in 1975 for example the UK inflation rate was 24.2% preceded by 16% in 1974 and followed by 16.5% in 1976. Effectively an item priced at £100 in early 1974 might have cost £167.85 by the end of 1976, over the course of less than three years people were expected to pay almost 68% more for material goods. That happened in this country less that fifty years ago, now I'm not suggesting that the annual rate of inflation will hit 24% in the event of a no deal Brexit, it could do but that figure seems unlikely. That said, inflation will most certainly rise significantly higher than its rate today and sterling will most definitely take another hit in terms of value. As a result you can expect that £60 in your pocket to have much less purchasing power than it does today.

I've deliberately focused here on one of the often perceived negative aspects of access to the single market, as I believe a Leave voter in 2016 might reasonably have done. What I haven't outlined are some of the benefits we gain from access to the single market, of which there are many. In the most simplistic of terms, we have tariff free access to the single biggest market in the world. We can import and export goods and produce that we know meets the high standards of the EU, we can do so without the additional levy that would be added in the form of taxation were we to trade under WTO rules.

Currently for example the EU tariff on food products and beverages imported into the EU under WTO terms is 21% of the value of the shipment. That's quite a significant figure. Do we really think British beef can remain competitive in Europe with an additional 21% tacked on before even getting near the consumer. Thats ignoring the fact that the price would likely have to increase for export due to Sterling being further devalued against the Euro. It's not unreasonable to expect a piece of British beef that currently costs ten Euro in France to cost fourteen Euro in France in the event of a no deal, needless to say that additional four Euro is of no benefit to the British farmer as he gets the same value in sterling as he is getting today. This is just a single example of one of the many benefits we gain with access to the single market, there are many more however this is not intended to be a lesson on the single market and how it functions. I merely wanted to point out some of the related facets of the four freedoms to help demonstrate the mere tip of the iceberg in terms of how our EU membership can and does benefit society as a whole.

I opened this chapter stating that Brexit has been an exercise in revisionism. Those who claimed we would continue to have access to the single market but we would not have to pay for it have since eaten their words. Literally every few days the prime minister appears to backtrack and promise one thing to the Remain MPs within her party and the polar opposite to her Leave supporting backbenchers in the European Research Group and the DUP. The same has been true over the past two and half years, remember how we definitely, under no circumstances were going to have a general election in 2017? How did that particular promise work out.

The biggest mistake made by the Leave campaign was to try to take an extremely complicated decision and make it black and white. As a means to an end from their perspective that was the correct thing to do, since they won. But in reality the process of leaving the EU is and was always going to be much much more complicated than anyone in the Leave campaign would ever care to admit. That's why a great deal has become a mediocre deal and a mediocre deal is threatening to become no deal at all. If we leave the EU without a deal then history will not judge them well.

Imagine jumping out of a plane without knowing if the parachute works. That's what some people voted to do when they voted to Leave on the 23rd of June 2016. To take that same analogy one step further I believe that if we crash out of the EU on the 29th of March without a deal, then at least some proportion of the people promoting such an outcome will effectively have decided to jump out of that plane without even knowing what a parachute was, and in doing so they will have taken the rest of the UK with them.

6
THE PROTEST VOTE

On the night of the EU referendum I became someone I never thought I would be. I sat up most of the night watching the results come in. When the Sunderland result came in I started to worry. A traditional Labour stronghold, voting for an outcome driven by the far right within the Tory party and UKIP. As I continued to watch the map slowly turn blue my fears were realised. Large swathes of England had voted to Leave. Every local region in Scotland voted to Remain as did most of Northern Ireland. Most local regions in Wales had voted to Leave but the most striking aspect that hit me was the fact that England voted to Leave in such numbers. As the most populous country in the UK we were headed toward a victory for the Leave campaign.

If the traditional Labour strongholds could not even push back against the Tory driven attempt to remove ourselves from the single largest trading bloc in the world then we had little hope. I truly believe that one of the single biggest factors in driving the decision to Leave was the fact that the official Remain campaign was led by a Tory government which had spent the previous six years chastising the population with extreme levels of austerity. The result was an entirely disenfranchised electorate, many of whom simply decided that the best way to stick it to the government was to go against them in the referendum. That's why the PM and Chancellor resigned off the back of a losing campaign. It was their fault, if they had went the other way and been backing Leave we may have ended up with an entirely different result. When places like Sunderland voted to Leave it was akin to Turkeys voting for Christmas. It has since come to pass that the North East stands to lose the most in the event of a no deal Brexit. An area that's received a disproportionate amount of EU funding is set to have the biggest fall in GDP as a percentage in the entire country, the drop is estimated to be 16%, an unprecedented reduction in wealth. To put this figure into context, the UK as a whole suffered a reduction in GDP of 6.25% with the global financial crisis from 2008. We still haven't fully recovered and have had to deal with years of collective financial hardship as a result. If 6.25% can have the sort of impact we saw with austerity then I dread to think what 16% might look like. It's not just the north east either, though that region would be the worst affected according to predictions. Overall the Bank of England expect the UK's economy to contract by 8% in the event of no deal, incidentally in the event of a deal they expect it to fall by roughly 3%.

In recent weeks Nissan have confirmed that they now no longer intend to produce the next generation of the Nissan X-Trail in Sunderland. That might not immediately impact on jobs today, but it will absolutely mean that there will be fewer jobs at that particular plant in the future. Outside the EU, and potentially without the benefits afforded by the single market of tariff free trade in Europe, Britain simply does not hold the same appeal to such firms so their decision should not be surprising.

A recent report by the Social Market foundation has found that the single biggest reference point for a person's decision to vote Leave in the 2016 referendum was driven by individual personal finances and a person's perceived happiness in relation to the situation. People who were happy about their financial situation tended to vote Remain and those who were unhappy about their personal finances leaned towards Leave. That same study estimates that nine percentage points of the 52% Leave vote (three million votes in total) was made up of people disenfranchised with the system and revolting against the financial hardship inflicted upon them with the financial crisis and exacerbated by several years of austerity imposed on them.

The Tory government's failure to grasp the public's anger over their endless austerity driven cuts over the preceding number of years was one of the primary factors driving voters to rebel against the status quo. Understandably so - in impoverished areas despite all the talk of a strengthening economy and a reduction in the deficit, those people felt that things were passing them by. Someone struggling to get by in the north east of England does not care that the economy is flowing ever more freely in the south and in London. They felt so disconnected from Westminster that it might as well have been on a different planet. In such a scenario it's extremely easy to buck the trend, try to break the system and you might get a new system. I believe that's what a number of working class people across the country did when they voted against the government in the referendum. Such hopes however may be considered to be entirely dependent on which government was in place to pick up the pieces after Brexit. If for example the current government remain in place then the most likely scenario seems to be further cuts and austerity to cope with the financial implications of leaving. If however a more progressive government were in place then just maybe they might get their wish.

7
THE OVER 65s

It's been well publicised that there was a generational gap in terms of the demographics that made up the majority of the Leave voters vs the majority on the Remain side. In truth the only age groups which voted decisively to Remain were the 18-24s (approximately 73%) and the 25-34s (62%). The next age group of 35-44 year olds also voted to Remain, but only by a small majority at 52% Remain. Beyond that each age group voted to Leave in ever increasing numbers with the 45-54 age group voting in favour of Leave by a margin of 56% to 44%. The 55-64s went one better with 57% vs 43%. Moving on to the final voting group of the over 65s we have a more decisive Leave vote of 60% vs 40% Remain.

The problem for the Remain camp with the above figures is that the older people get, the more likely they are to vote and so it proved in the referendum, with voter turnout among the younger groups being far too low to make a difference and the older groupings coming out in force to vote enmasse.

I myself belong in that third grouping of 35-44 year olds, I have a young family and I would like to think I have at least half my life still ahead of me. That being the case it's difficult for me to put myself in the shoes of the fourth, fifth or sixth groupings I've listed above. In particular its difficult to envision myself as being over 65, at that point my life experiences will be different to those that I've had up until this point in my life. I'll have worked all of my life and will no doubt have seen many changes in my lifetime, I already have at the age of 37. I have no doubt that my opinions on various topics will ebb and flow as I get older, the general consensus if history is anything to go by is that the older an individual gets the more conservative they become in their viewpoints. I personally can never see myself being anything other than a moderate to far lefty, however that's not the point. When I'm 65 or above I'll have had almost double the amount of life experience that I have today. I'll have different priorities, hopes and fears. The same is true I'm sure of today's older generation, a hippy during the 1960s could be quite conservative in their viewpoints at this point in their life.

The entire premise of the last few chapters has been an attempt to put myself in the shoes of people who voted for Brexit for varying reasons. With the over 65s I understandably can't do that with any great degree of confidence. But speaking with various friends and family of that age group, and trying to form well rounded opinions, reading various sources, including newspaper comments sections, opinion pieces and even things like social media comments. I believe I've managed to get at least a basic handle on some of the motivations that helped to drive that older Leave voter in 2016.

Many older people I speak with feel disillusioned with society today. Things are unrecognisable to how they were in the 1990s never mind the 1940s, 1950s and 1960s. Technology is one of the biggest factors driving the changes we've seen. We've also seen the breakup of the British Empire from its peak, former colonies were handed their independence, Britain has joined the EU and now seeks to leave it. We've seen massive changes in societal norms and we've seen changes that people simply would not have believed would be possible sixty or seventy years ago. I myself look at schools today and often think that there is not a chance in hell that we would have got away with some of the things that kids get away with today. The same is true at home when I see children in the streets and am surprised at how little control their parents seemingly have over them. Kids are shaped not only by genetics but by their environment and their life experiences. Children today are much more difficult to insulate from some of the less desirable aspects of human nature. Things like social media and the internet, whilst being extremely useful from an educational perspective can also be incredibly damaging to young developing minds if used irresponsibly. As a result, violence and a lack of respect for adults and authority are at pandemic levels amongst our younger generations and that makes the art of parenting and doing that properly (if there is such a thing) ever more difficult for today's parents.

Each generation naturally looks at their own childhood, how things were when they were growing up with a certain nostalgia. I work in technology, I use it every day and I enjoy it. I grew up as one of the first generation of kids that played computer games. Yet I also enjoyed playing outside with friends and arguing with my parents when they wanted me to come in during the long summer evenings as it got dark outside. I think this was the perfect period in which to grow up as I got the best of both worlds, I feel lucky in that I genuinely wouldn't change my childhood. Of course I feel nostalgia towards my childhood, provided we had a happy childhood we all naturally do, it's literally built into us. As we get older however we take on additional responsibilities and all of the stresses that go with those responsibilities, so it's only natural that as we grow older optimism can sometimes turn to pessimism and we often become more sceptical or wary of change.

When I mentioned how difficult parenting is today because of the inability to shield and protect children from the big bad world, I firmly believe that to be the case. However on the flip side, today's generation of parents are much better off financially on average than previous generations, which is bound to make at least that aspect of parenting less difficult. Many people still struggle to get by financially yes, but basic facilities that we take for granted today, such as inside toilets, were not common back when my parents were growing up in the 1940s in Belfast. The same is true of many other aspects of modern life and convenience. The UK economy has diversified and become stronger over the intervening years to become the sixth biggest economy in the world today (it was the fifth biggest prior to the referendum) meaning that on average despite the hardship many families face, we are better off collectively in terms of finance.

Another aspect of daily life that's changed dramatically over the past fifty, sixty or seventy years are our industries. The jobs people do today are often vastly different to those a generation before and the generation before that. A large part of today's economy in Britain, up to 80% in total is based around services, that figure includes both knowledge based services such as IT, Financial Services and Education as well as other services including Retail, Health and Transport etc. Primary production and manufacturing still makes up around 18 - 20% of today's economy but that's a vastly different picture to the last century. Our current manufacturing and production output includes industries as diverse as construction, mining, pharmaceuticals and agriculture. Increasingly British manufacturing and the industries which thrived during the industrial revolution have struggled to compete since the dawn of globalisation.

More and more products are imported as they can simply be made to a higher standard at a lower cost by cheaper labour abroad and in many cases automation and robotics are playing a larger part in manufacturing. The resulting savings are often being passed on to the UK consumer with cheaper pricing. Textiles, toys and products in every category are largely manufactured in the far east and exported to the world, including Britain. The shirt on your back for example was probably made in China. The result of this rapidly changing landscape is that people who have worked all their life in a particular industry have often watched as those industries have either declined, became obsolete, seen increasing levels of automation or seen an influx of labour from abroad. Many of our industries are now propped up by EU citizens, whilst in some areas that may have resulted in increased competition for British workers, the simple fact of the matter is that without those EU citizens many sectors of our economy would now struggle to recruit.

Change is not something that people are often comfortable with. Familiarity is often synonymous with security and a change can breed both resentment, fear and excitement in equal measure. I've seen the world change dramatically during my 37 years so I can only imagine how different today's world feels to a seventy five year old born in the 1940s. Life has become easier in some respects, facilitated by convenience and technology but simultaneously life has become more difficult with many of our older generation feeling alienated by today's society. Changes to how we work, how we live, how we bring up our families and how we communicate are all factors.

It's easy to look at one of the most visibly different aspects of today's society, multiculturalism and come to the conclusion that this alone (and what contributes more to multiculturalism than the free movement of people) is what has helped to contribute to the downfall of society. I firmly believe however that is not the case and that progression and technology, whilst entirely necessary, are also partly responsible for that perceived downfall of society. Today's children are tomorrow's adults, the next generation will shape the future. Whilst I'm not looking forward to some of the challenges that lie ahead of me as parent, in an ever changing and ever more dangerous world, I accept that the world has to change, and hope that it does so for the better.

An often quoted perception amongst younger Remain voters is that the older generations voted to Leave to spite the younger generation. They had things more difficult than we do today so why should they care if the economy goes down the toilet with a no deal Brexit.

Whilst I don't believe that was the case for many older Leave voters, I do believe that there was the feeling that the triple lock on the state pension meant that an economic downturn as the result of a Leave vote would not necessarily have much of an impact on pensioners and the older generation. The triple lock guaranteeing that the state pension rises by the highest of inflation, growth in earnings or 2.5% annually, has however only been guaranteed until the end of this particular parliament and that may well be amended at some point in the future.

There is a common myth perpetuated that pensioners have paid their dues all of their lives and that money is there, in the pot for when they need it. In actual fact this is not at all reflective of how the government actually finances the state pension. In fact the money paid into the governments pockets by previous generations has ALL long since been spent, and then some. In simplified terms the government effectively used the last generations contributions to pay for their predecessors state pensions. The current generation of pensioners are not financed by 'pension pots' that they paid into all their life, that money is gone long ago. The government instead relies on today's real economy, along with long term government debt (in the shape of freshly issued government bonds) in order to finance todays state pensions, along with every other piece of government expenditure. Therefore the risk to pensions is just as real as the risk to every other aspect of our economy. Brexit will damage the UK economy, of that there is little doubt, the only question is how much the economy will be impacted. By the time my generation reaches retirement there may well be no concept of state pension. The age for pension eligibility is ever increasing, due to the fact that more of us are living for longer so it's not inconceivable that within the next thirty or forty years it may cease to exist altogether.

8
THE XENOPHOBE

One of the most common accusations levelled at Leave voters by Remainers is the "you must be racist" line. It's a quick retort that goes to the very heart of the referendum result in that many believe that free movement of people was the single biggest contributing factor to the Leave vote. It's certainly not the case that 17.4 million people in the UK voted to Leave the EU because they are racist, xenophobic or they hate all foreigners. What is not in dispute though is that a significant number of those 17.4 million voters did so for such reasons. There isn't much research in this area but it's plain to see that at least some people had xenophobic motivations both then with the vote to Leave, and now with the argument over soft, hard and no deal versions of Brexit. The UK is by no means alone in its xenophobic tendencies, unfortunately for the decent amongst us in society the far right are on the rise across Europe and the wider world. The Brexit referendum result and the US presidential elections in 2016 are both examples of how the far right and populism are changing our democracies.

In the last chapter I mentioned how difficult I found it to put myself in the shoes of the older generation. I'm not even going to try to do so with this particular grouping. I firmly believe that all men and women are made equal. The colour of your skin, your gender, the country of your birth, your wealth, your religious beliefs or your sexual orientation shouldn't matter in a decent and fair society. Unfortunately many have not yet reached that point, narrow minded individuals will continue to try to resist the winds of change which have seen our societies diversify for the better.

Parties like the far right National Front in France have seen a surge in popularity. Similarly the BNP and later UKIP saw dramatic rise in support in the years building up to the referendum, all based on xenophobic rhetoric designed to try to stir those darker elements in society in a surge of populism. I believe elements in the far right of the Conservative party in the UK along with the Republican party in the United States are moving in that direction also and have been doing so for a number of years now.

Tools such as social media provide echo chambers and a means of reaching the masses with articles and videos that can quickly stir up resentment and fear in people. Every time there is anything occurring in current events in the United States that helps support the current president's agenda, and quite often when that's not the case, a single tweet can be distributed to millions of people in an instant. Often the information in those tweets is at best less than honest, often significantly worse. The term fake news was popularised during the US presidential election in 2016 and subsequently hijacked by those on the right to claim that anything that goes against their viewpoint is therefore fake news. The truth could not in fact be further from that viewpoint. The term "alternative facts" was coined by a Trump advisor shortly after the presidential inauguration, when trying to present an argument against actual facts to put a more positive spin on a story. The real source of fake news was inadvertently being exposed in that moment.

An attempt to present what was in fact a lie as an "alternative fact." Right wing media outlets tend to over-sensationalise information at best and report blatant lies at worst. Tabloid outlets in particular in the UK are well known for this practice, often printing those controversial headlines to sell newspapers, safe in the knowledge that the subsequent retraction following a lawsuit or complaint will not be anywhere near as impactful as that initial front page headline. A quick Google search of the phrase "Wikipedia bans" in the UK will help to demonstrate my point if you care to read some of the suggested articles. Try it, it's interesting to see why such a call was made given the sheer amount of right wing propaganda this particular outlet deems fit for print.

The point I'm trying to make here is that throughout history it's been much easier to popularise a lie than it has been to debunk that lie with a less sensationalist truth. Social media and the speed with which fake news is able to go viral is like the traditional media on steroids in its ability go achieve that same goal. I believe that a small minority of those who voted to Leave genuinely, in the heart of their being, harbour racist and xenophobic ideals. I hope that's an appreciably smaller number than what those figures might appear to be on the surface. I do however also believe that the minority with those views have used the traditional media as well as social media to try to bring those opinions to wider society and in doing so may unfortunately be influencing otherwise inherently decent people who are either uneducated or easily influenced by such negative opinions.

Britain did not vote to Leave the EU because 17.4 million people are racists, yet perhaps a few hundred thousand actual racists managed to hijack the opinions of a significantly larger number of easily swayed people and that just may have had a significant impact on the result.

9
THE STRING PULLERS AND THOSE WHO SEEK TO GAIN

One of most basal of human instincts is that of self preservation. Tens of thousands of years ago early man had to literally fight for their survival. Today that instinct more commonly translates to financial survival and prosperity. Whilst we all have hopes and dreams that do not centre around money, that particular commodity is unfortunately what metaphorically makes the world go round. Those with enough financial resources often try to buy happiness, sometimes unsuccessfully. Yet we all live our lives in pursuit of the financial gain that will 'hopefully' let us lead the lives we want to live. Many of the super rich are philanthropists and whilst they may make money hand over fist in their professional endeavours, they also give back to society through charitable donations. Many of the super rich unfortunately do not fall into this category, they are motivated purely by financial gain, having already accrued more wealth than they could ever hope to spend in a natural lifetime.

A number of very influential Leave backers have much to gain from Brexit. Their families are not the families who stand to go hungry if or when food prices skyrocket in the event of a no deal Brexit. Likewise they are not the individuals who work in industries which will struggle and therefore face the prospect of redundancy post Brexit. Car manufacturing workers who have already seen investment dry up in that industry in the

UK (approximately £500 million invested in 2018 compared to £2.5 billion in 2015) are in line for that particular Brexit prize along with many other workers in many other sectors.

As an experiment, try to search online for current sitting MPs who stand to make money from Brexit, perhaps search for "who will profit from Brexit" if you glance through the first five or ten search results you will likely come across quite a few familiar names who just so happen to lead the charge in terms of supporting the decision to leave the EU, no wonder - they stand to make a fortune.

In addition to MPs a number of those who helped to fund the Leave campaign financially, often did so for extremely selfish reasons. I'll not go into specifics here for obvious reasons but there is a lot of information already available on this particular topic in the public domain yet not widely publicised in the media. Try another quick search on Google for "Brexit backer made money from referendum" and you'll see lots of stories that help support my opinion on this. Leave voters I would particularly encourage you to do this, and then come back and think about the motivations of some of these individuals. Why would someone back a campaign to Leave the European Union, help to fund that campaign, seemingly "in the best interests of the country" and then position their companies to literally profit from that decision, by betting that UK's economy would suffer and sterling would fall in the result of a vote to Leave.

In some cases as much as £200 million was made by some Leave backers who bet against the UK economy whilst publicly promoting Brexit as in some way good for the nation as a whole. In truth the opposite is true. Whilst those with the financial means to do so helped to persuade the country that it was in the national interest to Leave, a decision to Remain would have boosted sterling and helped to bring stability to hundreds of industries. If the UK had voted to Remain, those who helped fund the Leave campaign would have made millions in losses. As it was however they engineered a victory for the Leave campaign by convincing the masses that it was in the national interest to Leave, through illegally financed campaigns. In doing so they helped to condemn the UK to a downward economic spiral whilst making millions for themselves.

Part Two – The Effect

10
THE UNSUSPECTING EU CITIZEN BUILDING A LIFE IN THE UK

I've never lived abroad. My entire life I've lived on the Island of Ireland, I've been lucky enough to travel widely, both within the EU and further afield. I've never experienced anything particularly unpleasant when travelling. Plenty of people do but luckily I've been able to see a lot of the world without having anything difficult to deal with. Having never lived abroad I find it difficult to try to put myself in the shoes of a Polish, Spanish, French or Latvian citizen who's resident in the UK. As one of the most widely spoken languages in the world most EU nationals will at least speak some English before they made their way to resettle in the UK. Having the native tongue is bound to help when resettling in a new country. Many entire families have moved their lives to the UK and Ireland and now call these islands home. The majority of EU nationals who've moved to the UK help to contribute to society as a whole. They work for a living across many sectors, they buy homes, their children go to school and often grow up to consider themselves British citizens.

Following the referendum result the amount of anti immigrant sentiment in the UK has increased dramatically. That hasn't been limited to EU citizens, reports of racial hate crimes against Asian, African, middle eastern and in fact immigrants from every corner of the globe have been widespread. As I mentioned in a previous chapter the vast majority of those who voted to Leave did not do so because they are racist or xenophobic. I believe a small minority of those 17.4 million people who voted to Leave did so for such reasons, it is clear to see however that unsavoury minority have since felt they have the right to hijack the result in their name. They claim when making statements such as "We voted to kick you out", "Go home nobody wants you", "We won, hurry up and leave" and variants of each of those statements using much more colourful language, that they were speaking on behalf of the nation as a whole. Clearly that was not, and is not the case. Most Leave voters would abhor such statements and behaviour. But that has not stopped those who seek to speak for all Leave voters when carrying out such horrendous racial hate crimes against innocent individuals and families, simply because the victim was not born in the UK.

I mentioned previously how difficult it is for me to put myself in the place of an EU national having moved my family to the UK. When I try to imagine that though, I can't begin to fathom how horrifying it might be to have your family threatened or worse, simply because I wasn't born in the UK. Unfortunately that was, and is a reality for many immigrant families.

Imagine you had decided to emigrate to Australia five years ago, you did so legally, sold your home in the UK, uprooted your children, moved your wife and children to the other side of the world. Perhaps at the cost of not seeing your parents and extended family for years on end. All this simply to get a better job and have the opportunities that perhaps didn't exist for you in the UK, whilst your particular skill set happened to be in high demand in Australia. Then imagine a right wing government in Australia decided to have a referendum in which you had no opportunity to vote, despite paying more in tax over the previous five years than your Australian neighbor, who happened to be on benefits with no particular interest in working or paying any significant amount in taxes. Said neighbour happened to be particularly xenophobic with an ardent dislike for the British, and the English specifically. The referendum doesn't go your way, it was a referendum on Australian visa duration for immigrants without citizenship or permanent residency. You thought about applying for permanent residency the year previous but a family issue got in the way. Now your visa is potentially going to be ripped up and you and your family face deportation to the UK. You are now facing the very real possibility of having to turn your life and plans upside down. While you await the decision on your appeal your neighbour and his friends decide to openly intimidate and threaten you. You wake one day to the sound of an upstairs window being smashed, a brick thrown through a first floor window narrowly missed your babies cot, you went outside and discovered graffiti on the side of your home telling you to go home. All of this simply because you tried to make a better life for your family. You did so legally and the country which once embraced you with open arms was now rejecting you, for no reason other than the fact that you weren't born there.

The above hypothetical scenario may seem as extreme as it does horrendous but things just like this have happened in the UK, in England, in Northern Ireland in Wales and in Scotland. Individuals and families who once felt welcome are now living in fear under the threat of a relative minority who claim to be speaking on behalf of an entire country. Those racists and xenophobes claim that 17.4 million people are on their side. I imagine somewhere between 15 million and 17.3 million of those who voted Leave are most certainly not on their side, yet that matters little to the innocent family who now face a decision on how they want their future to pan out and in which country that future should be. The statistics vary on this but a large number of EU immigrants have decided that their country of origin looks like a much more welcoming prospect than a country being hijacked, or least under the threat of being hijacked by the far right minority.

Immigration into the UK from the EU has fallen over the past few years since the referendum, statistics released on the 28th of February 2019 showed it has now hit a ten year low. People no longer feel welcome. Without immigration from the EU many businesses and the farming sector would struggle. I'll elaborate on that particular point in a later chapter but I for one feel that the UK as a whole will most certainly suffer without hardworking EU citizens making valuable contributions to countless sectors, paying taxes and helping to support our economy.

11
THE BACKSTOP AND THE ELEPHANT IN THE ROOM, IRELAND

Ireland, the island that I have called home my entire life. It's a very different place today than it was twenty years ago, thirty years ago and beyond. We've known peace on this island now for over twenty years. In 1994, 1995 and 1996 the paramilitary organisations declared ceasefires as pre-conditions to talks, those ceasefires faced various setbacks but in 1997 and 1998 were renewed and the talks that followed ultimately lead to the signing of the Good Friday Agreement on the 10th of April 1998.

As I mentioned in the foreword my generation hasn't had to deal with the troubles for as long as our parents and their parents did. I hope and pray that my child never has to know such times. Brexit is, regardless of what anybody in the Conservative party claims, a massive risk to peace on the island of Ireland. If a hard border were to be re-established, dividing communities and in some cases even next door neighbours then that border will ultimately become a target.

The reason that the Good Friday Agreement has been one of the most successful international peace treaties in recent history is the fact it allows a certain status quo to be maintained while old wounds heal and the catholic and protestant communities integrate much more so than they did in previous years. This is the world I want my child to grow up in, where religion doesn't matter and people just get on with their lives, treating good people how they deserve to be treated and not letting historic grievances trouble our present and our future. The return of a hard border in Ireland threatens to blow much of that progress away. One of the key points in the Good Friday Agreement was the fact that it helped to acknowledge the importance of identity to Northern Irish citizens on both sides of the religious and political divide. Northern Irish citizens are therefore free to hold both British and Irish passports and claim both British and Irish identity. The removal of all NI/ROI border infrastructure, allowing people in Northern Ireland to travel freely was therefore an important step in respecting nationalists affinity with the South. Unionists were safe in the knowledge that North would continue to be governed from London and remain part of the UK. Over the last twenty years it's been hugely successful and much of society has learned to move on. It's for this reason that the Northern Irish border and peace in Ireland have become the single most contentious issues in the negotiations with the EU. To potentially throw away twenty years of peace and progress would be a tragic waste for the people on this island.

One of the points I made in the foreword was the fact that even if every person within Northern Ireland had voted to Remain in the referendum on the 23rd of June 2016, collectively as a nation the United Kingdom would still have voted to Leave. UK wide 17,410,742 people voted to Leave the EU in June 2016, 16,141,241 people voted to Remain, a difference of 1,269,501 which is by no means an insubstantial number.

Northern Ireland's estimated population in 2016 was 1,859,000 people, its electorate in 2016 was 1,260,955.

Inexplicably (in my eyes) in NI we had the lowest regional turnout at 62%. Of those who actually voted in Northern Ireland 55.8% voted to Remain, whilst 44.2% voted to Leave. When turnout is factored into the equation and the votes were actually counted 440,707 individuals in Northern Ireland voted to Remain whilst 349,442 voted to Leave, a difference of 91,265 votes, again not an insubstantial number. UK wide however those figures barely make a dent. Even with a 100% turnout in Northern Ireland, if every single individual in NI had voted to Remain in the EU then the numbers nationally would differ slightly but not enough to swing the vote. In such a scenario (albeit an unrealistic scenario) the total vote numbers nationally would stand at Leave: 17,061,300 vs Remain: 16,970,035. Which as a percentage leaves us at 50.13% Leave vs 49.87% Remain, closer but not enough to make a difference.

For the sake of completeness if that scenario were to be reversed, meaning that every eligible voter in Northern Ireland voted to Leave then the Leave campaign would have had a more comfortable figure nationally at 53.86% Leave vs 46.14% Remain.

These figures are stark when you consider the fact that Northern Ireland is the only part of the United Kingdom with an EU Land Border. We therefore stood to be at the forefront of any future frontier yet the people in Northern Ireland were ultimately unable to affect the overall result nationally. When that fact is considered contextually with Ireland's history and the conflict which needlessly claimed many innocent lives, it seems ludicrous that Northern Ireland effectively had no say in its future. No way of ensuring the ongoing peace we have enjoyed in Ireland since the peace process and the Good Friday Agreement.

At this point I appear to have created a game whereby instead of quoting individuals or citing specific resources I let google do that for me. The next search I want you to type into google is "Brexit Secretary didn't read". You might then be surprised to learn that one of our many Brexit secretaries when questioned by the Northern Ireland select committee admitted to not having read the Good Friday Agreement. This is somewhat unbelievable given that the Good Friday Agreement and the prevention of a hard border in Ireland following Brexit is the single biggest issue in the negotiations with the EU thus far. Afterall parliament voted to back the proposed withdrawal agreement if the backstop were to be removed from the equation. So this single biggest stickling point in the negotiations is heavily influenced by the Good Friday Agreement, an international peace treaty no less. You might potentially excuse this fact if the document was hundreds of pages long, however it's not. The Good Friday Agreement is only thirty five pages long, it might have taken perhaps an hour or two to read. Yet the very individual trying to negotiate the terms of the UK's exit from the EU did not take the time to read up on the single biggest obstacle to that negotiation. I find that nothing less than staggering.

Economically Northern Ireland is curious, we cost the UK more to run and maintain than we collectively bring into the UK's Treasury in terms of taxes etc. Effectively it costs the UK to maintain control of Northern Ireland. Economically England, Scotland and Wales would be better off without Northern Ireland. As part of the Good Friday Agreement terms were put in place to allow the possibility of Irish Unity at some indeterminate point in the future, if the majority north and south so desired. I personally do not believe that there will be a United Ireland in my life time. If a referendum were called tomorrow on the subject I for one would not vote in favour, simply because I feel it would lead to a civil war and I don't want my child growing up in the environment that my parents had to endure with innocent people being killed simply because of their religion. Conversely one of my best friends is a Northern Irish protestant, he has said to me on many occasions that in the event of a hard Brexit he would vote for a United Ireland simply because he feels the economic impact of Brexit could be so stark that he and his family would be materially worse off. This was an unexpected development but it turns out to be a relatively common theme with others I have spoken with on this topic. The largest political party in Northern Ireland, the DUP wholeheartedly oppose the backstop in the current withdrawal agreement. The main reason they fear the backstop is that maintaining frictionless trade and travel within Ireland to help protect the peace process, would be at the cost of adding a few new checks to the existing checks done at ports between Ireland and Britain. Effectively adding an additional barrier to the existing barrier posed by the Irish sea. This understandably stokes fears within the DUP that it could bring us one step closer to a United Ireland, it may well potentially do that. However in my opinion and that of the friend I mentioned above who votes for the DUP in local elections, the potential chaos of a hard Brexit, or worse still a no deal Brexit would arguably bring that possibility more than one step closer due to the economic ruin in which we would find ourselves and the daily hardship that would place on family finances.

Northern Ireland receives a substantial amount of EU funding, not least through organisations such as Invest NI whom receive a significant proportion of their funding directly from the EU. That particular organization helps to support local business in Northern Ireland as well as bring inward investment from huge multinational companies. Bringing with them high quality, well paid jobs into the country and in doing so helping to really support the local economy. The fact that Northern Ireland is one of the less financially secure regions in the UK really means that we cannot afford to simply give up this inward investment and pretend that won't have a significant impact on us all. Within days of the referendum result recruiters in Northern Ireland were already reporting negative impact such as pauses on individual recruiting projects they had in the pipeline. With companies subsequently wary of committing, that may prove to be the tip of the iceberg. Northern Ireland, along with areas in the North East of England and Wales etc stand to be some of the worst hit regions financially as a result of Brexit. Northern Ireland should expect a reduction in GDP of roughly 11% in the event of no deal. Surely not a situation anyone in this country wants us to face, yet a near certainty following a no deal Brexit.

As tensions begin to rise in the run up to the 29th of March all sides are looking to try to leverage whatever they can to help push their individual agendas. That is how negotiations work. Some of the latest suggestions from the Brexit supporting right in the Conservative party however have pushed the boundaries lower than we might have expected.

One leading Brexit supporting Tory MP suggested in December 2018 that the UK could use the threat of no deal to bargain against Ireland with regard to the backstop. A substantial amount of Irish trade including food comes in through the UK and Ireland's economy could be set to contract by as much as 7% in the event of no deal. The fact that the UK's economy would contract by over 8% in the event of a no deal seemed to be irrelevant. Now the reaction to this in the Irish media was a bit more creative lets say than it probably should have been. Claims were made that the British wanted to effectively starve the Irish again, harking back to memories of the famine in the 1840s during which one million Irish people died and around two million emigrated in order to survive. The then British prime minister apologised in 1997 for the British role in the famine yet in this particular case no threat was made to starve the Irish rather it was being used as a negotiating tactic. What I find disturbing about this though is the fact that it was essentially a case of suggesting if the UK is set to go over the cliff with a no deal Brexit (entirely of its own choosing) then we are taking you with us in reference to Ireland. Nobody wants a no deal Brexit bar around fifty or sixty far right Brexiteers in the Tory party, there are six hundred and fifty MPs in parliament (six hundred and forty three if you factor in the fact that Sinn Fein do not take their seats). Yet we seem to be ambling ever closer to that nightmare of a no deal scenario at the behest of less than 10% of parliament. In the event of no deal the UK will suffer the most economically, closely followed by Ireland and the EU as a whole to a much lesser degree.

The current impasse in parliament is due to the Irish backstop. Despite the backstop being the brainchild of Westminster rather than the EU, the UK now seeks to have it removed from the withdrawal agreement. Yet the UK government has said they are committed to no hard border in Ireland to protect the Good Friday Agreement and peace in Ireland.

Presuming they achieve this seemingly impossible goal and there is no border in Ireland, how then do they propose to control free movement of people? At present any EU national can legally fly into Dublin without issue, that will continue to be the case after Brexit. What then prevents them from getting on a train in Dublin and being in Belfast less than two hours later. Subsequently on a plane from Belfast and in London two hours after that. Absolutely nothing as things stand. Millions of EU nationals already live and work in the UK. They don't currently have ID cards to indicate that they have permanent leave to remain in the UK. Are the government planning on rolling out ID cards for all EU nationals in the next few weeks stating that they are free to remain in the UK (in line with the UK promise that existing EU immigrants will be given indefinite leave to remain)? If not then what prevents an individual from travelling to the UK via Ireland from Spain, France, Poland or Latvia on the 30th of March following a no deal Brexit. Suddenly it appears that one of the main motivating factors in the Leave campaigns success has been rendered redundant as there is simply no way to police it. Either that or the UK government are being duplicitous in their claims that they intend to honour the Good Friday Agreement and protect peace in Ireland, given the history between the two nations, unfortunately I suspect the latter will be the lesser of those two priorities.

12
THE NHS

I've spoken to many working in the NHS who were angry about the referendum, particularly at the fact that the Leave campaign attempted to hijack the nation's vote and do it in their name. As I mentioned in chapter three, many voters wholeheartedly believed that if we voted to Leave the EU an extra £350 million would be available for the NHS every week. That money patently could never have been given to the NHS since it didn't exist in the first place. Another pain point that often angers those in the NHS is the mismanagement and misappropriation of funds. As we saw in that chapter the government have a lot more available to them in the treasury than the majority actually realise. What we pay into the EU every week is a small fraction of our Gross National Income, the NHS budget in contrast is already a huge proportion of national expenditure, it has to be due to sheer breadth of the services it has to provide. A major problem however is the fact that despite aspiring and claiming to be one of the best health systems in the world, and despite the NHS already having a substantial budget, the government are not willing to provide the necessary funds to help sustain acceptable levels of service. They certainly don't provide an appropriate budget to back up the claim that we have some of the best healthcare in the world.

Our government insists that the NHS has sufficient budget and that money needs to be used more wisely and efficiently. I agree to a certain extent with the latter part of that previous sentence. I do not however agree that the NHS has sufficient budget, many years of Tory austerity has seen to it that accident and emergency rooms are staffed with skeleton crews. In my local hospital recently in the accident and emergency department, one of the largest in the entire of Northern Ireland, I was informed by nursing staff that there was one single doctor on duty. We'd been waiting for several hours already and when we did see the doctor we were informed, by the doctor herself that she was a junior doctor and did not have any training in the particular area where we needed assistance. Subsequently we were told to go home because there wasn't the expertise available to help deal with the issue. Surely this was and is a patent demonstration of how lacking at times our NHS can be. I don't in any way blame the junior doctor but I do blame the system that leaves a junior doctor without sufficient training in charge of one of the largest A&E departments in the country.

Surely then, regardless of inadequate budget and staffing levels, of which there is clearly a major case to be made. If we admit that there are efficiencies to be had within the NHS, it's the government who are ultimately accountable for that NHS and therefore any mismanagement and/or poor use of funds is on their watch.

I mentioned in chapter four how bureaucracy plays a significant role in some of the problems people perceive with Brussels and the EU, I agreed with that stance to an extent. In the case of the NHS however any Bureaucracy, of which there is a significant amount, is not in any way shape or form the doing of Brussels.

Rather it's our own government as the custodians of the NHS. When doctors and nurses are complaining about the amount of needless paperwork that is carried out at the expense of patient welfare. Or that the amount of time spent on that paperwork prevents doctors and nurses from actually seeing and treating patients, then we know that something has gone awfully wrong with the system.

A single prescription costs the NHS £45, The NHS spent over £70 million in England alone prescribing paracetamol in 2016, yet the drug can be purchased in some supermarkets for 19p. Surely common sense should be used here, if a drug can be purchased by an individual for 19p then under what possible circumstance does it make sense for the NHS to spend £45 to achieve an identical result. The same is true of other similarly cheap, over the counter drugs such as Ibuprofen, which can again be purchased at a fraction of the cost in a supermarket. These are just some of the contributing factors which help to demonstrate that clearly the NHS can use it's funds more wisely.

We've all likely heard something or other about health tourism in the UK, that's non UK nationals travelling to the UK for medical treatment that they would not otherwise have received in their country of origin. Health tourism does exist, it's estimated that it costs the NHS between sixty and eighty million pounds per year, this is a huge number but when compared to the overall NHS budget of around £113 billion per year, the upper end of that estimate comes to a paltry 0.07% of the overall NHS budget. Now consider the fact that you are statistically much more likely to be treated by a doctor or nurse who also happens to be an immigrant and that picture starts to look slightly different.

One additional aspect to consider is the fact that the majority of immigrants in the UK, and in particular those of EU origin tend to be younger. It's common sense that as we get older we are more likely to need to make use of the health service on a regular or semi regular basis. Older people get sick more often, and the impact of illness usually has a more profound effect on our bodies as we age. We take longer to get over things, we may not be in a position to look after ourselves at home, meaning that hospitals stays are more likely to last longer as we age. It's fair then to say (and studies have been carried out in this area) that younger, generally healthier EU immigrants are much less likely to avail of the NHS than the average British national as we are an aging population. Couple that with the fact that the majority of those who come to the UK from the EU tend to do so to work, and therefore pay taxes. And it becomes easy to see that really the effect of EU nationals on the NHS, taken at balance has and is extremely positive when considered fully. This is at odds with the perspective hyperbolised by the right wing media to advance their narrow minded anti immigration agenda.

One of my best friends happens to have type one diabetes. Anyone familiar with the disease will be aware that it's not related to age, or being overweight, or lifestyle choices, those are all factors with type two diabetes. Rather with type one diabetes there are genetic links which predispose an individual to the risks of developing the disease. It can come on suddenly and without warning. The consequences of type one diabetes are that your body cannot produce enough insulin, without insulin our blood sugar levels spike and remain at dangerously high levels indefinitely if left untreated. Therefore those suffering from the condition have to actively manage their blood sugar levels. They achieve this through a combination of dietary management, quick release insulin to deal with short term spikes following a meal and longer acting insulin to ensure that blood sugar levels remain stable overnight. Take too much insulin and you run the risk of going into a diabetic coma, take too little insulin and your blood sugar levels will remain too high. Whilst the latter of those extremes is less dangerous in the short term it can lead to serious long term effects such as blindness, loss of limbs and reduced life expectancy. Neither of those scenarios is particularly appealing and therefore diabetics need to constantly monitor their blood sugar levels throughout the day and night to ensure that it remains within the optimal range.

At the minute the majority of the insulin we use in the UK is imported from the EU. In the event of a no deal Brexit, there will simply not be sufficient supply to meet the demands of the approximately 3.7 million people living in the UK who have been diagnosed with either type one or type two diabetes. An estimated 4.6 million people have the disease with roughly 0.9 million people living with the diabetes yet not being aware of that fact. When I mentioned that type one diabetes is genetically linked, with type two diabetes lifestyle choice put some of us more at risk than others. At the minute approximately 12.3 million people in the UK have an increased chance of developing diabetes due to their weight and other factors. That's an awful lot of people who should be concerned that in less than four weeks time we may not have enough of this literally life saving drug to go around. So much so that some individuals are literally stockpiling their own personal supply. I recently read an article whereby an individual had an entire double fridge, stocked full of a combination of slow and quick release insulin. He'd been building the supply over the last number of months to ensure that in the event of no deal, he at least has enough of the drug which keeps him alive to last for the next year or so. Beyond that I'm not sure what happens to that particular individual. If insulin is no longer available on demand then over a number of years more and more people will have diabetes linked complications and guess where they will end up? In our hospitals, putting ever increasing pressure on an NHS that's already at breaking point. Statistics show that over the last few years the amount of people waiting for more than four hours at A&E has gone up by 600%, a frankly astonishing figure. If that's not a service in crisis then I don't know what is.

Insulin represents a single drug which we will struggle to supply in the event of a no deal Brexit. I happen to know about that example because of my close personal friend who has the disease. Yet there are many hundreds of other drugs and supplies which we will have difficulty providing if the worst comes to the worst and on the 29th of March we fall off a cliff edge and out of the EU.

Another rather important example is that of radioactive isotopes, those used in cancer treatments, guess where the majority of those come from currently? If you guessed the EU then you guessed correctly. The more you care to dig into this particular topic the scarier this situation becomes, as much as we tend not to like reading about bad news, I would encourage everyone to do so. Better to be informed and own our decision rather than bury our heads in the sand and pretend everything is just going to magically work out fine.

The scariest single aspect to my mind regarding the chronic underfunding and mismanagement of the NHS, is that the NHS is in some respects relatively efficient in comparison to other healthcare systems in wealthy nations. The current government however seem intent on underfunding the NHS to breaking point. At which point their desire to move further and further towards privatisation and the selling off of parts of the NHS to Health Care companies in the United states looks more justified. Do we really want to move toward a model whereby people sometimes have to choose between treatment for cancer or keeping a roof over their families heads? I may be borrowing a plot line from the first series of Breaking Bad, but these are the very real decisions that families often have to make in the United States on a daily basis. It could potentially be something we have to deal with in the UK at some point in the near future if the NHS continues to be underfunded in the way it has been by our current government.

Recent reports have estimated that austerity has cost 120,000 lives directly due to the £7,000,000,000 in cuts to Health and Social care under the Tory government. That's an awful lot of people we've lost because the government decided to underfund our National Health Service.

In 2018 a former health secretary suggested that patients can simply sit if there aren't enough beds in hospitals. At that point we really should have got the message being delivered to us all, that the Conservative government have such a blatant disregard for the people they claim to serve that they will happily throw those doctors and nurses on the front line in our NHS under the bus. Quite possibly, just to add a little salt to the wound, it would likely be a big red bus with some sort of brazen lie printed on the side. Maybe something about an extra £350 million per week going to the NHS following Brexit.

13
THE FARMING INDUSTRY

Chlorine washed chicken and hormone injected beef. These are just some of the products that our farming industry may have to compete with in the event of a no deal or hard Brexit. Why anyone would particularly want to consume the aforementioned products is beyond me, but the Brexiteers in our current government want to pursue trade deals with the United States that would see such products flood the UK market, at the cost of British products which meet EU standards on food quality, safety and animal welfare.

The laws which govern our food standards in the UK are inherited from the EU. There are currently bills passing through parliament to replicate the existing EU legislation on food safety into UK legislation post Brexit. There has to be to keep open the possibility of any continuing or future customs union with the EU. If the UK did not replicate the existing EU legislation then the EU could simply not allow the import of UK products that do not meet EU standards. In the event of no deal or a hard Brexit however anything is possible and any prospective trade deals to be had with the United States would almost certainly contain food produce that does not come close to EU standards. The EU simply will not allow the UK to become a backdoor into the EU for substandard or unsafe food products and in my opinion that is by no means an unreasonable stance to take.

Our farming industry is one to be proud of. There is a reason why the meat you buy in a supermarket so proudly labels itself as British or Irish beef and makes a deliberate point of making a big deal of that. Over the last forty years the British farming industry has spent time and money ensuring it meets the high standards set out by the European Union in terms of food hygiene, quality, animal welfare and importantly food safety.

To suddenly have to pay tariffs on already tight margins prior to export into the EU, or to be undercut by cheaper less safe products, from the United States for example could spell the death knell for the industry. That combined with the fact that our farmers receive substantial financial subsidies from the EU, and those will cease to apply post Brexit means that farmers already struggling with tight margins will not be able to cope financially. The Northern Irish Ulster Farmers Union is a regional farming body which has confirmed that they simply could not compete, under any circumstances in the event of a no deal Brexit. How could they be expected to when they would face those 21% tariffs on food imports that I mentioned in chapter five. The only viable alternative would be to sink to the lowest common denominator. If UK farmers had to try to compete with sub-standard and potentially unsafe imported products then the only way they could realistically compete would be to lower their own standards, undoing the progress made over the last forty years and potentially endangering us all.

Another aspect of Brexit which will hit the UK farming industry particularly hard is the prospect of staff shortages. Without freedom of movement many farms will struggle to get staff in the numbers they require because, simply put, UK citizens do not want to do the work that EU citizens will do without question. That may sound patroniing but its a simple fact, wages in a number of EU countries are lower than those in the UK. As a result a seasonal job paying minimum wage, for example picking strawberries, is often attractive to EU citizens. They may only intend on staying in the UK for a number of months to carry out that seasonal work (which British citizens are seemingly unwilling to do in many cases), before returning to their country of origin for several months of the year. Many who claim that "they are stealing our jobs" are the very type of individuals who are unwilling to do those jobs themselves and are much happier to simply exist on benefits. I realise this is a generalisation and that is not always the case, but it often is the case and the point must be made. Often however there are other more legitimate and understandable reasons why UK citizens are unwilling to carry out the sort of farming jobs, and in particular seasonal farming jobs that EU citizens are much more willing to contemplate. Farming by its very nature is highly seasonal. Often people will be expected or need to relocate to remain employed in such a sector and UK citizens are understandably reluctant to relocate their families for short term contracts, preferring to seek longer term employment, in sectors which offer stability and potential long term career prospects. In many cases EU citizens have no such concerns if for example they are simply in the UK for a few months to make significantly more money than they can make in their country of origin. Farming often involves heavy and/or difficult, stamina sapping activities, sometimes in difficult conditions. The workforce in the UK has largely moved away from physical labour and whilst it obviously still exists, the type of physical labour UK citizens tend to carry out these days has moved on from farming in many cases.

I recently read about one particular example of this phenomenon in action, whereby a UK farmer suggested that of his last several thousand job applicants only three of those were from British citizens. Without EU citizens that farmer would simply not have enough staff and his crop will quite literally rot in the fields. Surely not an outcome anyone would have aspired to when they decided to leave the European Union, yet in the event of no deal or a hard Brexit it will certainly come to pass.

14
THE BANKERS AND BIG BUSINESS

Right now businesses up and down the country are in a state of panic over a potential no deal or hard Brexit. In truth many businesses have been insecure for the last thirty months since the referendum. Initially fears were somewhat allayed by all the government's promises that there would be a deal and Brexit wouldn't harm British business. As time ticks along though with the default position being no deal, and little prospect of the government emerging from years of incompetence to get a worthwhile deal over the line, Business leaders are growing increasingly nervous and making decisions that will negatively affect the country for years to come.

Worryingly a phrase that's being bandied about on an ever increasing basis by average people is "Who cares about business anyway". At the end of the day we should all collectively care about business, since the fewer healthy and profitable businesses we have, the fewer jobs they have to offer. With fewer jobs available there will be less paid into the treasury through taxes. What that eventually means for the rest of us is more people relying on benefits and the rest of us paying more in taxes to help fund it.

Nothing in the above paragraph is anything more than basic common sense, it's obvious and worrying in equal measure. Yet many seem oblivious to the fact, despite what so many businesses in so many sectors have been claiming for over two years now.

There is a reason why the government offered assurances to various businesses in the wake of the referendum, "there would definitely be a deal", "we will compensate you for any losses you make as a result of Brexit etc". The government essentially offered Nissan a bung of £60 million to get immediate assurances that their next models would be built in Sunderland. Nissan made that promise at the time but in February 2019 they pulled out due to Brexit uncertainty and falling demand for diesel vehicles in Europe. As I mentioned in chapter six areas such as Sunderland will be decimated in the event of no deal, Nissan pulling investment is merely the tip of the iceberg. Without access to the European market, Sunderland, and the UK as a whole, becomes a political and economic backwater with very little upside for those multinational corporations. Eventually many will up sticks and leave.

Another big player in the UK car manufacturing industry is Ford. They currently employ thirteen thousand people in the UK, making engines and transmissions for cars which are built in the EU. Ford have said that they face losses of eight hundred million dollars in 2019 alone due to Brexit. Under World Trade Organisation (WTO) terms there are currently 4% tariffs on components and 10% tariffs on cars coming into the EU. Under a no deal or hard Brexit scenario Ford for example would face even greater losses than those listed above. Since components for use in their engines, and eventually the engines themselves cross the channel into the EU several times back and forth during the manufacturing process. On each occasion in the event of a no deal or a hard

Brexit an additional 4% would be levied on the cost of those components. Eventually once the cars themselves are fully assembled in the EU, they would then face an additional 10% levy upon import back into the UK. It's not unrealistic to see a scenario whereby Ford may cumulatively see an additional 30% or 40% levy on their cars being sold in the UK if we follow the current path we are treading towards a cliff edge Brexit and no deal. Ford would not see a single penny, yet consumers would be expected to pay 40% higher prices. Despite the fact that the average family in the UK would have less disposable income. According to a study by the Resolution foundation in early 2019, the average household in the UK already have £1500 less in spending power compared to projections made prior to the referendum. The estimates following Brexit vary based on the type of exit, but in the event of a soft Brexit, a hard Brexit or a no deal scenario the average families income takes ever increasing hits.

Another multinational firm which has recently spoken out on the subject of Brexit is Airbus. A few weeks ago in January 2019, with two months to go until the potential cliff edge of a no deal their CEO said that in such a scenario they may have to relocate their UK operations. Airbus happen to employ fourteen thousand people in the UK, they also help support four thousand smaller businesses in the UK within their supply chain. Suddenly the prospect of fourteen thousand job losses in a single company, which is already a stark figure becomes potentially an unprecedented threat to an additional four thousand businesses.

The three companies that I've discussed here are all huge in terms of scale, but Brexit not only has the potential to cause severe disruption to those multinational firms. It also has the potential to devastate smaller businesses in their supply chains as I highlighted with the Airbus example.

Independent small businesses, with no exposure to multinational firms supply chains will also face unprecedented difficulties. The EU represents our single biggest trading partner in the UK. Both in terms of import and export markets. If we leave the EU without a deal or under the terms of a hard Brexit, then many small businesses will cease to exist. Quite simply because they will have lost tariff free access to their largest customer base.

The institute of directors have stated that a no deal Brexit would force at least a third of all businesses in the UK to consider moving at least some, if not all of their operations abroad. The UK workforce currently stands at thirty five million, the vast majority of that in the private sector (roughly twenty seven million people). The prospect of one third of that private sector workforce being at risk of potential job losses due to relocation outside the UK is hard to fathom. 17.4 million people may have voted to leave the EU but they did not vote for a no deal Brexit which puts nine million jobs at risk.

One aspect of the impact Brexit has already had on the UK is the opportunity cost to business. This refers to the lack of investment in certain sectors which otherwise would have occurred, had the UK opted to Remain in the 2016 referendum. It might mean lost contracts, reduced sales, foreign investment not coming into the country which would have otherwise. The Nissan case above is just one such example, all over the country contracts are being torn up. Projects are being delayed and foreign investors are simply biding their time, essentially waiting to see where the chips fall with regard to Brexit.

Such lost investment coupled with reduced spending power etc has seen the UK's economy slow down at a dramatic pace since the referendum, when compared to other advanced economies. The economy has been diminished by some 1.1% (or for emphasised impact £23,000,000,000 yes that's £23 billion) in terms of GDP since the referendum, compared to Office of Budget Responsibilities own pre referendum estimate. If the mere threat of Brexit can have such a dramatic impact on our economy, I dread to think what the event itself might bring in the coming years.

In these dangerous times our politicians should be trying to strengthen our ties with the large businesses who help to bring security, in the form of well paid jobs to thousands of UK workers, and potentially tens of thousands of jobs in their supply chains. We need to ensure that these businesses are able to continue their UK operations to minimise the risks to our economy and, taken at an individual level to ensure that people keep their jobs. It struck me then as rather puzzling when a Tory Brexiteer decided to react aggressively to the Airbus statement about potential relocation from Britain. That politician responded with comments on how his father had fought in the war and had never given in to a German, and that he wasn't about to either. All this due to the fact that the CEO of Airbus happens to be a German National. This was never going to be a helpful comment in the grand scheme of things. Rather it serves only to demonstrate the sense of entitlement some people in the UK harbour, and a certain level of national nostalgia for World War Two and the fact that the Germans were defeated. Frankly such comments belong in the past in satirical comedies such as Dad's Army. Not in serious discussions on the future of the country and our prosperity, or lack thereof for decades to come.

I mentioned in chapter one how I once worked in an investment bank, albeit in IT rather than banking. Following the global financial crisis investment banks weren't popular amongst the general public, they still aren't today. The big investment banks primarily based in London do however bring a significant amount of money into the treasury. London is currently the financial capital of Europe and, by extension the capital of the largest single market on the planet. That's rather a nice position to be in when the vast sums are considered. An entire book could be written, and many probably have been on the impact Brexit will have on the city and the financial services industry but suffice to say it's impact will be huge.

As much as the everyday man or woman in the street may not like it, the big investment banks have a huge part to play in terms of our society as well as global power and influence, the fact is that they do. That's why we constantly heard the term "too big to fail" in relation to those same investment banks back in 2007. The basic premise behind this is that banks do astronomical amounts of business with each other and with the wider economy as a whole. The entire banking industry was like a house of cards back then and whilst it isn't so vulnerable today, severe financial shocks can have a huge and far reaching impact. Entire trading desks are dedicated to foreign exchange, commodities, stocks and shares, government bonds, equities, options, futures and treasury. All of these functions have the potential to reach deep into other areas of the global economy and indeed our everyday lives. Many people may believe the misconception that when you put money in the bank it's stays there. This however is patently not the case. Under a system known as "fractional reserve banking" banks retain as little money as they are legally required to in the form of liquidity and the rest of the money is put to work.

Trading is essentially an extremely well informed and statistically driven form of educated betting. In the most simplistic of terms, what happened with the global financial crisis in 2007 was the gradual realisation that subprime mortgage bonds weren't quite as valuable as they were once thought to be. Banks with large exposures in those bonds were effectively facing huge losses and as a result those banks themselves became less creditworthy. A vicious circle ensued whereby a bank with severe subprime exposure had a knock on effect on all of their creditors i.e other banks which owned debts from that original bank. The trouble with this though is that practically all of the banks hold positions (I.e trades) that are linked to each other and the same was true back in 2007. So as each of those banks started to unravel their positions in the subprime mortgage market, they identified more and more exposures to potentially bad debt. As a result all of those banks then became less creditworthy and the entire industry became ever increasingly nervous. The reason the banks were too big to fail was because if one fell then they might all fall due to the negative knock on effects and the risk of debt having to be written off.

When Lehman Brothers filed for bankruptcy in 2008 it was a nuclear bomb to the industry. It triggered a domino effect whereby countless multinational banks had to be bailed out by their governments to prevent a global economic meltdown. Due to those government interventions the damage was limited, we had a global recession, but it did not quite reach the levels of the great depression of the 1930s. Nonetheless the effects of the global recession which began in 2008 were felt by many and in some cases those effects are still being felt today.

Another aspect to consider is that banks not only trade with each other on stocks and shares, currency and commodities. They also trade on government bonds. These are bonds written by governments all over the world, to effectively finance things now that they can't quite pay for yet. New bonds are written today to pay off the dividends on bonds which were written twenty years ago and longer. This is a never ending cycle of debt. It's the equivalent of me or you maxing out twenty five credit cards and getting twenty six new credit cards to pay off the old ones. The fact that interest will be due meaning that we have to borrow ever increasing amounts.

Almost every major developed nation is severely in debt through the use of such government bonds. Take the United States of America for example. The supposed richest country in the world and by far the largest single economy in the world, also happens to be the most indebted nation in the world. The US has a National debt of almost twenty two trillion dollars (including inter-governmental holdings) as of the end of 2018, staggering figures by any standard.

In the UK, our national debt figure stood at £1.78 trillion as of Q1 2018. Whilst that may seem small compared to the equivalent figure for the USA, it's by no stretch of the imagination a small figure. Quite the opposite it's the equivalent of what we would send to the EU in the next 195 years at our current rate of EU contributions (£9.1 billion per year). That's 195 years based on what we send to the EU, not including what we receive in return by way of EU funding. If we were to factor those figures in also, to look at Net EU contributions, it would increase that 195 year period dramatically.

That top line figure of £1.78 trillion has to be financed. The majority of us have at some point in our lives purchased something on credit. We are therefore fully aware of the concept of credit, and interest payments. In order to service the current national debt, the UK pays out £30 billion per year in dividends (effectively interest). That's almost three times what we send to the EU annually, before taking into account what we receive in terms of EU funding. The interest figure alone amounts to roughly 2% of GDP or 5% of the total government tax income.

We are not alone in this situation. The vast majority of countries on earth have a national debt. The world quite literally runs on credit with most countries spending a lot more money than they can generate through their economies.

Why is any of this important in the context of Brexit you might ask. Quite simply as a demonstration of the reasons why growth in our economy is so important to every aspect of modern life. The reason why the UK government pursued such aggressive policies of austerity from 2010 onwards was essentially their way of attempting to balance the books.

The deficit, of which we heard so much about in the news, was essentially the fact that the UK budget was more than we could afford. The amount of money coming into the treasury was lower than the amount we were spending. As such the national debt continued onwards and upwards. The UK's national debt has risen from £1.01 trillion when the conservative government took power in 2010 to £1.78 trillion by the start of 2018. When we look at the overall national debt figure and compare it to GDP representing the overall size of our economy, and therefore our ability to afford such debt. The UK national debt has risen from around 40% of GDP at the start of the recession caused by the financial crisis to around 90% of GDP by the end of 2017. This is a demonstration of how badly a recession can hit the national debt, essentially due to the fact that government tax receipts subsequently reduce and welfare spending then increases as a result of more people being out of work.

Such a model can not be sustained indefinitely yet there are different approaches to be had in an attempt to deal with such a problem. Rather than decimating public spending in an attempt to reduce the amount going out in terms of government expenditure. A more positive approach may have been to try to stimulate the economy to bring more revenue in by way of tax receipts. The fact that a recession which saw our economy contract by 6.25% caused our national debt to balloon so rapidly serves as an important warning. Models predict that UK GDP will contract by 8% as a result of a no deal Brexit. Can we really afford a recession of that scale and the resultant impact that will have on our national debt? Annual interest of £30 billion could conceivably double within a few years and make the £9.1 billion we send to the EU every year look like small change in comparison.

It's at this point that I can make my actual point in relation to banks and their importance to the UK economy. Quite simply the financial services industry is a tremendous generator of revenue for the country as a whole. To take London as the single greatest contributor, the amount of money traveling through the capital of the largest single market on earth is frankly staggering. The vast majority of that money flows through London because its within the EU and the single market. Last year the financial services industry contributed approximately £75 billion to the treasury in tax receipts, 10.9% of the total tax receipts for the country as a whole. If we leave the single market then next year and every year for the foreseeable future that figure takes a nosedive. What that will likely mean for me and you is an awful lot more austerity, likely much more aggressively implemented and over a longer period of time. The poorest in the country will suffer most. Effectively anyone who voted to Leave because they weren't happy with their financial situation are akin to turkeys voting for Christmas.

The UK's economy is, simply put, not prepared for a cliff edge Brexit. It would quite literally devastate entire communities and cause social and financial hardship for millions of people for decades to come. On this particular occasion the government really need to open their ears and listen to those bankers and big businesses who have been warning them for two years now of this calamity waiting to happen, in less than a months time, if we leave with no deal or a hard Brexit.

15
THE SCIENTIFIC AND RESEARCH COMMUNITY

Science is massive in the UK. It may not always be very visible in terms of the public consciousness or in the news, but right now there is critical scientific research being carried out in this country and we just so happen to be very good at it. Science tends to be international by its very nature. Almost every scientist in history has based their work on the shoulders of those who went before. Cooperation and knowledge sharing are the very cornerstones of how scientific research is conducted worldwide.

Ranked internationally the UK is rated as second worldwide for the quality of the scientific research being carried out within our institutions, surely something to be extremely proud of. Many of our universities are known worldwide and steeped in history. These are just some of the reasons why we have so many international students, including many from the EU desperate to secure places in those universities. In terms of talent, the UK attracts some of the best minds from across the continent and indeed the world. Many of those international students, not only those from the EU have felt marginalised since the referendum. We are also now seeing fewer applications from those top drawer international students than ever before.

It's not just in terms of talent that we face a downgrade following Brexit either. The UK has been very successful over the last number of years in terms of qualifying for and winning grants for science and research from the EU. A large proportion of the funding going into those sectors in the UK comes directly from Brussels via EU funding. Some funding programmes ran within the EU are actually open to countries outside of the EU but at least half of those programmes are EU exclusive in terms of their eligibility. The European Research Council (ERC not to be confused with the much less scrupulous ERG) alone have already granted prestigious grants worth 1.29 billion to the UK in terms of funding for important scientific research. In the event of a no deal Brexit the UK stands to lose around £500,000,000 per year in terms of EU funding. UK institutions will no longer be eligible for around half of their current funding.

Scientific research in practically every field is carried out in the UK every year. Some of the most important work worldwide in terms of cardiovascular research and cancer research is carried out within the UK. But often that work is carried out in collaboration with our EU partners. If you were to walk into any lab in the country you would almost certainly find scientists of several nationalities. Lots of the best scientists in the world make their way to these shores but we also work internationally with laboratories within the EU and further afield in collaboration on major clinical trials.

Within the scientific community papers and findings have traditionally been peer reviewed as the base measure to determine reliability and authenticity. That is still the case however, more recently the 'Citation Impact of Scientific Research' has become the defacto method to determine the quality of research and its authenticity. Essentially the more times a particular article or author is referenced the more likely that research is reliable. Recent studies have shown that UK research scores extremely highly when compared internationally using this particular metric. Crucially however in a study carried out by the Centre for Science and Technology Studies at Leiden University, British medical research carried out in collaboration with our EU partners scored significantly higher (1.98) than research carried out in the UK alone (1.6). When compared to research carried out in the EU without the collaboration of the UK (1.37) or the worldwide average (1.0) we can start to build up a picture to demonstrate just how important UK/EU cooperation is, particularly in regard to some of the most important medical research being carried out in the world today.

If the above paragraph highlights anything, it's that the best work is carried out when the UK and the EU collaborate. The fact that such a lot of that collaboration just so happens to be in research into Cardiovascular disease, which is still the single biggest cause of death in the UK (and worldwide) makes that continued cooperation all the more crucial. Cancer research is another field whereby UK/EU collaboration is crucial to the success of that research. Cancer statistics vary but the general consensus is that collectively different types of cancer were accountable for between 25% and 30% of deaths in the UK last year. During my childhood I remember a statistic which stated that one in four people will develop cancer in their lifetime, that statistic is now one in three. The fact that average life expectancy has improved is obviously an important factor in this but worryingly, the latest research has determined that one in two people are now likely to develop cancer at some point in their life.

Many cancers today are treatable, early detection methods and treatment are improving all the time. But central to that progress are the clinical trials and scientific research being carried out in the UK with the EUs cooperation. If that fact is not enough to make people realise how important that ongoing collaboration is then I'm not sure what will.

Scientific cooperation with the EU was one of the twelve key areas the UK government originally set out to try to seek a consensus with the EU at the start of the Brexit negotiations. The importance of such cooperation cannot be overstated. Yet the hard Brexiteers still seek a a no deal Brexit, and with a no deal Brexit that cooperation becomes immeasurably more difficult.

16
THE LORRY CAR PARK IN KENT

To revisit my good old sourcing game from google again, another particularly interesting search term to use would be to search for the text "Brexit secretary didn't understand". On one of the first suggested articles you might find a reference to the fact that one of our three Brexit secretaries (in under three years) *"hadn't quite understood the full extent of this" "but if you look at the UK and look at how we trade in goods, we are particularly reliant on the Dover-Calais crossing"* this being due to the fact that the UK was a *"peculiar geographic economic entity"*. That peculiar nature of the UK, is apparently the fact that it's an island, very peculiar indeed. Some might even suggest that most people learn about islands in primary school but apparently some of our politicians were not held to the same standards in school as the rest of us.

The above paragraph represents a worrying trend if we try to unravel the threads that make up the Brexit story thus far. It seems some of our leading Leave backers and in fact the individual whose very job it was to try to negotiate the terms of the UK's exit from the European Union, don't understand the complexities of leaving or even understand the simple fact that as an island nation. We are reliant on the Euro Tunnel and the Dover to Calais ferry crossing for imports and exports. We are living in precarious times indeed.

The government's no deal Brexit planning has recently included the decision at the end of 2018 to give out lucrative contracts to shipping companies to help with the expected backlog in the event of a no deal Brexit. In one such case they even gave a multi million pound contract to a company which didn't actually have any ships and had never operated a shipping service. They happened to spend an estimated £800,000 prior to getting that deal in place on background checks and consultant fees etc. This is somewhat unbelievable, with only a few weeks to go until the 29th of March. Following the obvious public and political backlash the government climbed down and cancelled that particular contract around six weeks later. Presumably due to the fact that there was no possible way that company, with their imaginary boats would be in a position to fulfil that contract on time, prior to the 29th of March. Such lack of foresight and inability to perform the most basic levels of research (despite spending eight hundred thousand pounds) prior to handing out a multi million pound contract, to my mind simply beggars belief.

In more recent developments Eurotunnel who have also operated a shipping service, have since opened proceedings to sue the UK government. This due to the fact that the aforementioned deals were secretive in nature and they were not given the chance to compete. The reason this legal challenge had legitimacy is due to the fact that government contracts of this nature are supposed to be put out to tender. This gives companies the opportunity to compete on a level playing field when trying to win such lucrative contracts. With the legal challenge from Eurotunnel hanging over their heads, and that likely to make it to court where the government would almost certainly have lost. The government instead decided to pay Eurotunnel £33,000,000 to make the problem simply go away. The UK taxpayer effectively having to pay for the government's botched handling of the no deal preparations.

The reason the former Brexit secretary was highlighting the "peculiar" nature of the UK's geography and that fact that the Dover to Calais crossing is of particular importance was due to the fact that in the same speech he referenced the reason why leaving the EU with a deal to ensure frictionless trade was so important. To quote *"that is one of the reasons why we have wanted to make sure we have a specific and very proximate relationship with the EU, to ensure frictionless trade at the border"*. That sentence taken in isolation makes perfect sense. What certainly does not make sense is how only a few months later the same group of Leave supporting MPs are now pushing for a no deal Brexit which would cause utter chaos at the borders.

Over the last number of months we've heard lots about the potential lorry car park in Kent in the event of no deal. The government staged a practice run for this eventuality in January this year, whereby eighty nine lorry drivers were paid £550 to effectively reroute to a Kent airfield. All this in aid of a dry run to help understand what may happen in the event of a no deal. The main problem with this particular 'test' was of course it's ridiculous scale. By comparison an average of ten thousand lorries pass through the port of dover every single day, so parking eighty nine lorries on an airfield just doesn't quite cut it.

The very latest developments with this particular piece of farcical Brexit 'planning' is that the government made an announcement on the 4th of February 2019. They are now planning on simply allowing incoming lorries to pass through our ports without any checks at all. In fact lorries will be allowed to provide simplified customs declaration up to two hours before a Ferry crossing to the UK or travelling through the channel tunnel. The customs duty on any individual shipment would then be payable up to a month after the journey. The rationale behind this would be to help to prevent undue delays on incoming lorries. And the subsequent chaos that would cause for a number of our industries which are reliant on "just in time delivery". Supermarkets and the like have particular vulnerability in this area as any delays with imports would prevent us from effectively importing a number of everyday goods and produce. The UK currently imports approximately 41% of our fresh fruit and nuts and around 76% of our fresh vegetables from the EU. Those are vast numbers when we are talking about produce with limited shelf life. We are particularly reliant on Spain closely followed by the Netherlands. With our climate in the UK we simply don't have the conditions required to grow a number of the daily staples we expect to see on our shelves in supermarkets. Measures such as the above are simply required in order to reduce the risk of food shortages, even with measures such as this in place they will only have limited effect as importers will still have to pay significant tariffs and those costs will be directly passed onto consumers.

During the referendum campaign the slogan "take back control" was everywhere. The Leave campaign deliberately used such a generic throw away slogan in an attempt to be all things to all men. In one instance it might have meant taking back control of our borders, a moment later it meant taking back control of our laws, it sometimes meant taking back control of our trade. In truth Brexit is unlikely to deliver satisfactorily on all three of those areas barring a no deal Brexit. However in the event of no deal, taking back control will be the least of our worries. If we leave without a deal and in a months time the above 'planning' around delayed customs checks and unchecked inbound lorries at our ports has came to fruition then the ability to control our borders might be a tricky one to implement. What is rather more likely than 'taking back control', is that we'll end up with a smugglers paradise which could just so happen to coincide with the biggest influx of illegal immigration in decades. Due to zero control at ports and thousands of lorry drivers who might be a bit more inclined to assist an illegal immigrant due to the fact that those lorry drivers lives will have been made immeasurably more difficult by Brexit.

The problem of delays on imports may potentially be partially mitigated by the waving of customs checks at our ports. That unfortunately will not have any effect of the delays we'll likely have with exports. As previously mentioned ten thousand lorries pass through Dover per day. The fact that in the event of no deal every single one of those lorries will have to be meticulously checked on the other side of the channel will drastically slow down ferry turn around times and still potentially back up the channel tunnel France bound all the way back to Folkestone and into Kent. In order to protect the single market, Europe simply has to perform customs check on inbound shipments at their point of entry into the EU. If the UK leaves with no deal or is not part of a comprehensive Customs Union with the EU, then that frontier will be Calais for the vast majority of British exports. That lorry car park in Kent could be out of control within days of no deal. I hope the people of Kent are ready for it because the government most certainly is not.

17
THE POLITICS

I deliberately left the politics to the end because everything that I've written up to this point has in some shape or form had a political cause or effect. Whatever the outcome of Brexit it will be on our politicians' heads. The Conservative party have fought an internal civil war for years over Europe, the Eurosceptics in the party moving ever further toward the far right.

Since we joined the EU, every successive leader in the Conservative party has, to varying degrees, had to fight to try to keep the party united on Europe. Most of those leaders have been pro EU or moderates who could see the merits offered by EU membership, a few have been Eurosceptic themselves and tried dragging the party and their policies further to the right.

Brexit and the mess it has become, was and is entirely the product of Tory self interest. For forty years the party have been divided by the European question, the former prime minister called the referendum for entirely selfish reasons, to make his life easier managing his back bench. Donald Tusk (the president of the European Council) has confirmed that the former PM didn't believe he would get a majority government when he pledged to call a referendum in 2013 and felt that the probable outcome of the 2015 election would likely be another coalition with the Liberal Democrats, who would surely block a referendum on Europe. Thus kicking the can down the road on the European question and giving him a free pass in terms of EU membership.

The current prime minister doesn't want to be the person in charge of the Tory party when it almost inevitably splits, hence the continued attempts to satisfy the far right ERG element within her own party. This despite a softer customs union, or better still a Norway style Brexit being the much easier options to get through parliament, which would also conveniently remove the need for the largest stumbling block i.e. the backstop. The one problem with this though is that is that it opens up the contentious issue of Free Movement of People, one of the EU's four freedoms and the pillars around which it's single market is structured, simultaneously one of the biggest motivating factors driving the Leave vote during the referendum. Were the PM to pursue single market membership or a permanent customs Unions the Conservative party would almost certainly suffer an unprecedented split.

The biggest mistake the former PM made when calling the referendum was to try to pit a complex truth against a simple lie and put it to the public as a binary decision. Given the Brexit campaign and the 2016 US election it would appear that complex truths versus simple lies is the new way politics is seemingly done. With little or no downside for those purporting the lies (i.e. in both cases the liars won). Despite us now living in an age where there is more information available to more people than ever before (i.e. on the internet), people simply don't check and often take the blatant bare faced lies purported by some politicians as facts. For that reason we now have a president in the white house who, according to the Washington Post publicly portrayed mistruth as fact fifteen separate times per day throughout the course of 2018, the number of falsehoods he peddles behind closed doors must surely be a staggering number.

In the case of the Brexit referendum however, the former PM was firmly in the Remain camp and therefore he set himself up for a fall in that he was on the side of the complex truth, inherently much more difficult to sell. The Remain campaign told the story of how beneficial EU membership is to the UK, and how detrimental it would be to leave but they fought an unfair battle when set against extremely basic and obvious lies told by the Leave camp which were much more appealing to the man on the street. Just like the US presidential election, with the Brexit referendum it worked out well for those campaigning on blatant lies. Prime amongst the lies were the now mythical "We will get a great deal from the EU, it will be the easiest deal in history", "the NHS will get an extra £350 million per week", "sterling will be fine and we won't see any inflation, it's all project fear" all of those blatant lies have since been debunked yet somehow a referendum was largely won based on those extremely obvious and simple lies.

Effectively at the minute a political game of chess is being played out in Westminster. We 'the people', are merely pawns, to be sacrificed so the would be kings and queens can become ever more wealthy and powerful. Those kings and queens aren't necessarily the politicians themselves (though in some cases they are). Often political policies and decisions are made in the interests of wealthy donors and financial backers, often times also those financial backers have influence and/or controlling stakes with the largely right wing media. Political lobbying is seen by many as a legal mechanism to effectively buy political decisions. This is the entire reason why the US president pursues a ridiculous apparent vendetta against our natural world and environment, relaxing fossil fuel regulation whilst simultaneously slashing the budget for the Environmental Protection Agency and putting a climate change denier in charge of that same agency. The only plausible reason to do this is to scratch the backs of the financial backers who put him in office. There is a brilliantly simple yet powerful demonstration which helps to describe this phenomenon by a recently elected NY congresswoman, if you search for "aoc dark money video" you'll find the clip, it's around five minutes long and I would strongly urge you to watch. I digress to climate change naturally as I believe it's the single biggest threat to our continued existence on this planet, yet that's the subject for another story.

To move back to the topic at hand with Brexit and the UK, I don't believe that political lobbyists necessarily have the same levels of influence in this country as they do in the United States, perhaps they do but just aren't as blatantly obvious about it. None the less campaign finance laws in the UK are designed to make it more difficult to buy elections, the biggest issue with this however is that the punishments for breaking those laws are not nearly punitive enough. The Leave campaigns in the Brexit referendum broke several campaign financing rules. Essentially the referendum was won illegally, yet the fines dished out for those breaches were tiny when set against the funding itself and therefore in real terms there is no significant consequence to illegally funding a campaign.

Unfortunately in the UK there is limited regulation of the press and again little consequence for those breaking the regulations that do exist, as a result another mechanism that's available to those who would seek to influence the masses and politics for their own financial gain. In the UK often the media is used as a tool to help to push the political agenda that suits their biggest shareholders interests, and this is yet another reason why we find ourselves in the current predicament. The body responsible for press regulation in the UK IPSO publish leader boards of UK newspapers by the number of complaints they receive, retractions and action taken against publishers. It just so happens that the 'top' performers on these leader boards (i.e. those promoting the most falsehoods) just so happen to be some of the same publications which vociferously support Brexit.

Moving back to the strictly political arena, the vast majority of the blame for this mess lies at the doorstep of the Conservative party, we are however beginning to reach a point whereby Labour are no longer blameless in this. They now appear to be assisting the current PM in her relentless mission to kick on towards the 29th of March, unchecked and unaccountable. Labour are guilty of facilitating the PM by refusing to whip the party to vote for amendments ruling out no deal and by failing to stand by the position they set out at the Labour party conference to back the call for a second referendum in the event they were unable to secure a general election. They are now moving towards that position, but I fear it's going to be too little too late.

The largest parties in the UK are playing these political games at the expense of the future prosperity of the country. The Conservative party are trundling along, effectively sleepwalking towards no deal, their reasons for doing so are obvious. The Brexiteers, as things stand are effectively set to achieve their ultimate goal, a no deal Brexit, whilst the more moderate within the party and the PM are pandering to them for fear of splitting the Conservative party indefinitely and irrevocably. Labour are afraid to back a second referendum for fear of alienating voters in Leave constituencies. Understandably so, given that 75% of marginal Labour seats are in Leave voting areas, that's effectively 75% of marginal seats that the Tories might hope to win were Labour to publicly back a second referendum as their official position and therefore be seen to be blocking Brexit. The term 'party before country' has never been more apt. Yet there comes a point, and that point has long since passed, where party politics should no longer matter. As it stands we are on track, full steam ahead towards a no deal Brexit, despite the fact that probably less than one hundred MPs desire such an outcome, the other five hundred and fifty plus MPs desire some softer form of Brexit or to Remain, yet those one hundred or less MPs on the far right of the Tory Party are holding the government, their party, parliament and ultimately the country to ransom. They are being allowed to get away with it because the leaders of the two largest parties are afraid to stand up and make a difficult call.

Across the water in Ireland the two largest parties are also playing political games. The DUP, fearing the backstop as a potential first step towards a united

Ireland, are doing everything in their power to see it removed from the withdrawal agreement, despite the fact that the backstop in itself would see Northern Ireland in the unique position of having an open tariff free trading relationship with the EU whilst ensuring it retains the same status within the rest of the UK. Economically Northern Ireland would stand to do pretty well out of such an arrangement. There may have to be a few additional checks on products at Irish ports and those on the west coast of England, Scotland and Wales however the volume is not nearly as significant, and there hasn't been any talk of lorry car parks in Belfast, or Larne nor are there any such fears in Stranraer, Liverpool or Holyhead. That's because in terms of sheer numbers the amount of lorries passing through those routes is relatively modest in comparison to the numbers passing through Kent and into the main arterial routes at Dover.

Sinn Fein the second largest party in NI believe they are in a win win situation as things stand, with the backstop the status quo is retained and we ensure ongoing peace in Ireland whilst our economy wouldn't be nearly as badly hit as other parts of the UK. Despite their public position though, they are secretly revelling at the prospect of a disorganised Brexit and the economic catastrophe that would follow, for that, in their minds, would almost certainly accelerate the breakup of the UK.

In the event of a hard Brexit Scotland will inevitably call for another referendum on independence, this one however will succeed since the main argument against independence last time was that Scotland wouldn't be part of the EU if it were to leave the UK. That argument is now null and void as Scotland (like us here in

Northern Ireland) have voted to Remain yet are being dragged along kicking and screaming out of the EU by England. If Scotland leaves the UK at some point in the near future, surely an inevitability in the event of a hard Brexit or no deal, then that removes a massive block of former Labour voters which would be very scary for the rest of us in terms of future general elections.

If/when Scotland leaves the UK, given the fact that Scotland are currently a member state and therefore they already meet the strict criteria set out by the EU on standards etc, then the EU could accede their re-entry into the EU in record time. If nothing else to get one over on the rest of the UK and effectively say "I told you so". The main potential stumbling block that could prevent an independent Scotland from re-joining the EU would be the possibility of a Spanish veto. The reason Spain might object would be to prevent a precedent being set, one which those seeking independence in the Basque and Catalan regions in Spain might hope to follow.

If however Scotland were to re-join the EU, then an independent Scotland as part of the EU would be a vastly more prosperous place than the North of England a few miles away, an attractive proposition then for other regions of the UK to potentially break away from England since effectively it was only England which voted to Leave the EU by any significant margin.

Sinn Fein then, see such a scenario as an opportunity to achieve their ultimate aim. I for one still likely wouldn't vote for a united Ireland because I don't want my child growing up with a civil war hanging over his head, but plenty of people on both sides of the religious divide could likely be persuaded if it offered an instant route back into the EU, given the financial hardship many in Northern Ireland will face in the event of no deal.

The basic annual salary of an MP from 1 April 2018 is £77,379, due to go up to £79,468 from April 2019. MPs also receive expenses to cover the costs of running an office, employing staff, having somewhere to live in London or their constituency, and travelling between Parliament and their constituency. Funny then that many seem reluctant to "go against the will of the people" despite the fact that a significant proportion of 'the people' have since changed their mind on Brexit.

In recent polls 70% of Tory voters still want to Leave the EU, yet over 80% of Labour voters want to Remain. When figures are analysed collectively at a national level 56% of people would now prefer to Remain versus 44% of people who still want to Leave. These figures are merely opinion polls and as such they are fluid. Despite that Remain has held a substantial lead over Leave for quite some time now, ever since we started running into significant difficulties with the negotiations on the withdrawal agreement. Never has that lead been so stark though as in recent polls.

The current PM however knows which side her bread is buttered on, she is clearly trying to keep the Tory electorate happy despite the fact that in the country as a whole 56% of people would now choose to Remain if given a binary choice. The public are now much more informed than they were on the subject of Brexit prior to the referendum, therefore how can ensuring that it's still what the people want be going against democracy. Given the fact that even the most strident Brexiteers now know that there are no unicorns or magic pots of gold at the end of the Brexit rainbow.

On the subject of our current PM, she was once considered to be moderate, due to the fact that she was a former Remain supporter, when tested however she is proving every day that she values one thing over all else. Political survival from a personal perspective and the Conservative party over the country. Her former position as the Home Secretary, even more obsessed with immigration than many of her hardline Brexiteers ensures that she is of the opinion that the Leave vote was irrevocable proof that the country as a whole wants to end free movement of people, hence the dismissal of a Norway plus style arrangement with the EU. Another former position she held was that of the Conservative party chairman. The prospect of splitting the party is therefore beyond contemplation. The risk to the Conservative party is however that for short term gain i.e. delivering Brexit like they said they would, they would ultimately face decades of pain as nobody could ever trust them to be competent again, given the calamity that will ensue in the event of a hard Brexit or no deal.

One good thing may still come from this Brexit shambles, it could well see a reboot of our political system. Politics tends to swing from right wing to left wing and back again in waves, with people often blaming the government of the day for their problems. Often those politicians and their policies may well be to blame. My fear is that the swing globally towards the right is a worrying trend that might be hard to reverse as the very policies which keep the average working person in their place, coupled with the extremes of social media and the echo chambers it encourages are effectively dividing us further than ever before.

There is hope though, in this country the Labour party currently has a more left wing leader than they have had in decades, I don't agree with all of his policies but inherently I see the desire to do good and try to build a system that works for everyone rather than just the top 1%, to my mind that can be no bad thing. There is a downside to his extreme leftism however, in that it occasionally alienates some of the more moderate centrist members of the party.

I wrote this chapter on the 17th February 2019, I had originally written that I didn't see the risk of a split in the Labour party being anywhere near as high as the likelihood that the Conservative party will surely split at some point in the near future, in any scenario with the exception of no deal. Whilst writing this book however, events continue to overtake me despite Brexit seemingly standing still as our politicians continue to try to square a circle. Whilst the two main parties are effectively afraid to contemplate any option that may offend Leave voters, politicians within both parties are beginning to mobilise and upping the rhetoric as we approach the 29th of March. As such the day after I originally wrote this chapter seven Labour MPs officially quit the party to form the independent group within parliament, two days later they were joined by another Labour MP and three moderate Conservatives. All eleven of those MPs are disillusioned with their former parties insistence on delivering Brexit whatever the cost to the nation, they favour a people's vote that would ensure that current opinions in the country are considered. This mindset is seemingly at odds with the Tory party leadership in particular who are treating an advisory vote two and a half years ago as sacred, despite the fact that opinions have largely moved on, and the reality of our Brexit options are radically different to those sold to the people by the Leave campaign. The eight Labour MPs who have defected have done so for similar reasons, in that they believe now is the time to put Brexit back to the people since the government clearly can't deliver what they promised. The Labour leadership are, in my opinion biding their time and being cautious with their official move to back a second referendum, they inch towards it at a snail pace and I don't believe they will whip their MPs to vote in favour should it come before the house of commons. In my opinion this approach is overly cautious because whatever the political cost, the damage to the country is too great to risk a no deal scenario.

When I originally wrote this chapter I did not believe there was a risk of a breakaway faction of moderate Tory MPs from the party, rather I focused on the fact that many in the ERG, on the extreme right of the party will consider moving to UKIP, the newly formed Brexit party, or they may well form their own party in the event of anything other than an extreme hard Brexit or no deal. Personally I believe that such a split in the Conservative party would be one silver lining to the disaster that has been Brexit. I abhor their selfish trickle down economic policies which are inherently designed to make the rich richer and keep everyone else in their place. The Tories like many right wing governments the world over are effectively a bunch of reverse Robin Hoods, they rob from the poor to give to the rich.

With both the main parties then potentially at risk of more significant splits than those which have occurred already, at some point there becomes room for a more centrist party to bring us back to something approaching equilibrium and normality, that group may have now formed with the eleven MPs making up the independent group. At the moment the group is too small to have a major impact but with additional defections they may become more influential. Events may continue overtake me. In the remaining weeks leading up to the 29th of March more moderate MPs may quit the Conservative and the Labour parties. That may have the desired impact and help to prevent a no deal Brexit however fundamentally which party existing MPs sit within in Parliament matters little, their respective positions on Brexit and the parliamentary arithmetic is what matters. More than enough politicians want to avoid a no deal scenario, they just need to develop the backbone to stand up for their convictions and prevent the country sinking into an economic black hole entirely of its own making.

Many people are not fans of the concept of centre left or centre right governments. The argument that they please neither the right nor the left is based on sound logic. I however would argue that whilst they may not fully please anyone at least they don't provoke the extreme reactions from the opposite side of the political divide that far left or far right governments tend to elicit.

That last point is crucial, because today more than ever, people are split, entrenched in their particular position on Brexit, on Right vs Left, on Immigration, on Populism vs Libertarianism. Polarized viewpoints are only enhanced by social media and the echo chambers those sites create. Algorithms on these sites show you content that you will be more inclined to pay attention to based on the content you have previously engaged with, and how you engaged with it. It isn't necessarily things that you 'like' either. Those posts that provoke a furious reaction still provide traffic and potential shares nonetheless (albeit with an accompanying comment of your disgust). With traffic comes more advertising revenue and that is the root of the issue. These websites not only track the articles we read and the posts we like or dislike, they also track how long we spend on articles, how many times we revisit them, if we copy links and forward them, share them, retweet them etc etc. Many social media sites now know more about aspects of our personalities than we do ourselves.

With these echo chambers and rise of fake news we are seeing a global change in democracy as we know it. A piece of fake news can spread far and wide at an alarming rate and once that horse has bolted its difficult to contain.

The point I'm making here is that at the end of the day it's important to realise that people are allowed to have their own opinions in a democracy, we are lucky that we live in a part of the world where that's acceptable. My fear however is that with such divisive politicians at the helm, dividing and conquering the nation we are quickly moving away from such values.

THE CONCLUSION

I decided to write this book at the end of January 2019, it will be released in early March 2019 and could well be out of date within a week. This is a consequence of ***how quickly events are unfolding within the Brexit landscape***. I also mentioned previously how ***Brexit was seemingly standing still***, surely two sides of a dichotomy if ever there was one. Despite this I stand by both statements.

Whilst events are literally unfolding at a rapid rate in the run up to the 29th of March, those events are the desperate attempts from all sides, to ensure that their particular objective in relation to Brexit is met. A no deal Brexit or a people's vote. Withdrawal/extension of article 50 or the current withdrawal agreement getting through parliament and being put into action. As we approach the point of no return, business leaders are becoming ever more nervous at the prospect of no deal and are making themselves heard, meanwhile politicians try to hold their nerve hoping someone else will blink first. These opposing viewpoints are mutually exclusive in that only one group of people will achieve the result they desire, and all other efforts will in the end have proven futile. From this perspective significant events are occurring every single day, as we use the final two months of a twenty four month period (since article 50 was enacted) to try to come up with a solution. MPs are resigning, parties are splitting. Our International Trade Secretary is trying to desperately roll over some of the third country deals that he was sure the UK would be able to roll over in time for midnight on the 29th of March (current progress he has made on this front is six deals from a total of forty). These third country deals are trade agreements we have with non EU countries due to the fact we are members of the EU. They include huge trading partners such as Japan, if we exit the EU without a deal we not only lose our free trade agreement with our largest trading partner, the EU itself, but we also lose the benefits gained by up to forty other trading partnerships.

The reason such frantic attempts are now being made to prepare for Brexit, deal or no deal, is because our government effectively wasted the first twenty two months of that twenty four month period. It is here then where the statement that Brexit is standing still is appropriate. Our politicians and the PM in particular still aren't doing anything, they haven't done anything meaningful for two years. It's like they are trying to park a forty foot lorry in a standard multi-story parking space, trying to achieve the impossible from multiple different angles.

How many times and in how many ways must the PM and her negotiating teams be told the same things. Yet nothing seems to be going in, they continue ad-infinitum to go back to Brussels to try to renegotiate. Only to be told there can be no renegotiation, they go back to parliament to say there can be no renegotiation and are told to go back to Brussels to try to renegotiate. It's getting to the stage were Britain is literally the laughing stock of the world, self sabotage on a grand scale with our PM metaphorically running around like Benny Hill.

If this book is out of date within a week, one month or two months due to the ever changing landscape of Brexit, the majority of the content will likely still be relevant because ultimately I don't think that come the 30th of March the UK will have left the EU. I believe that the most likely outcome at this point will be an extension of article 50, despite the PMs insistence up until very recently that we will definitely leave the EU on the 29th of March regardless of how. Yet another u-turn to add to the many we've had from our PM over the last two years. I cannot see any situation which allows the UK to leave with a deal on the 29th of March, because no such deal exists, in reality no acceptable deal can exist. If we leave with no deal it will be by accident. Extension therefore seems the most likely course of events. That however will only delay things and at some point in the future we will be back at this point, staring down the barrel of a gun (no deal or hard Brexit) but afraid to walk away (remain in the EU).

Delaying Brexit will not be straightforward. As I've mentioned in previous chapters, the default position is that we leave with no deal on the 29th of March 2019. In order to get an extension on the two year period allowed by article 50 we need unanimous approval from each of the other 27 EU nations. It's likely that those nations would grant an extension but its by no means a certainty.

The Prime Minister has now suggested that on the 12th of March a second meaningful vote will be held on the current withdrawal agreement, it will almost certainly fail. She has also now suggested that on the 13th of March a vote will be held to temporarily take no deal off the table. This vote will almost certainly pass. On the 14th of March the House of Commons will then have the opportunity to vote to extend article 50 to delay our exit from the EU beyond the 29th of March 2019. This final vote will also almost certainly pass.

The crucial points the Prime Minister made when making her speech on the above proposed votes was that any extension should be short in nature to quote *"not beyond the end of June"*, and *"an extension cannot take no deal off the table"*. This then, is essentially a trap, designed to bring us closer to a sharper cliff edge Brexit in June. The PM wants to extend up to the end of June knowing that it would then become immeasurably more difficult to extend or delay beyond that point. Essentially forcing MPs to then choose between her deal or no deal.

The reason why an extension into June would present such a dilemma is due to the fact that by that stage the European Parliament elections will have taken place (in May 2019) and the UK will not have taken part in those elections. If those elections take place and the UK has not participated, then the EU will not countenance another extension beyond the end of June. Since that would effectively paralyze the European Parliament, which would then be unable to make decisions from the 2nd of July 2019. On that date the new parliament is due to hold its inaugural session and if the UK remains a part of the EU on that date, but the UK does not having any sitting MEPs (and therefore no representation) many legal experts believe that any decisions taken by the European Parliament would be open to legal challenge and therefore won't be binding.

Brexit therefore has the potential to render the European Parliament defunct, at least temporarily. It is for this reason that many in the EU will be understandably wary of granting any extension. They may consider a longer extension if the UK were to participate in the EU elections however that will almost certainly not have happened since the government are firmly on the path to leave whatever the cost and whatever the current public opinion.

The UK will still have one card up its sleeve were we to extend into June and not have taken part in the European elections. The European Court of Justice recently ruled the UK could unilaterally revoke article 50 should it desire. This would then not require approval from the other EU 27 nations, however such a move would then ensure that Brexit would be delayed by at least another two years, likely longer as regulations stipulate that article 50 cannot be revoked to simply be re-enacted again.

All of the above therefore then suggests that an extension to June seems likely. At that point we still won't have a deal because all of the same unsolvable problems will still exist. The UK continuing to try to square a circle by preventing free movement whilst protecting the economy, still attempting to achieve any meaningful Brexit whilst not sacrificing peace in Northern Ireland. Either we continue with access to the Single Market or we face a collective reduction of wealth that will make 2008 seem like a mere bump in the road. Many in Parliament won't stand for the former, the country as a whole will never forgive our politicians if they go for the latter. This however appears to matter little to our politicians. The PM will run the clock down to the wire again in June, knowing that MPs will have to vote for her deal to avoid a no deal scenario, any extension then is simply a stay of execution.

This particular period will be a curious chapter when future generations judge the history of this country. They will look at the decisions made in 2016 and those being made today and will struggle to comprehend the collective economic suicide of a nation that we are heading towards.

The Bank of England's latest set of figures predict that in the event of a no deal Brexit we will see inflation move towards 6.5%, unemployment is expected to reach 7.5% and house prices are set to fall by 30%. Leading Brexiteers have moved on from their favourite catch phrase over the last three years when faced with information or research or even factual evidence that in any way conflicts with their agenda. No longer do they talk of *"Project Fear"* they now speak of *"Project Hysteria"*. They claim that any negative economic impact of Brexit will be short term in nature, only to follow that in the next breath by stating that "short term" in this context means roughly fifty years. The Bank of England however have little to gain by providing misinformation, rather theirs is a neutral perspective and many of the predictions they have made up until this point have proven remarkably accurate. Again not so if you listen to those same leading Brexiteers. Those same leading Brexiteers who stand to make millions in personal wealth should the UK leave the EU. It's almost difficult to decide who is more likely to be telling the truth, my money however would be on the Bank of England.

Many countries have experienced a great deal more hardship than Brexit will ultimately inflict on the UK, however in the vast majority of such instances that hardship was caused by famine, natural disasters, war or the regime of a dictatorship. In at least the first two of those scenarios the outcome almost always cannot be influenced by those who suffer, in the latter two scenarios often that is the case also. Never in recent history has a nation undertaken an exercise in self harm quite like the UK over the past three years.

All of the potential upsides of Brexit promoted by those who believe we should leave the EU at any cost are shallow in nature and/or extremely easy to debunk. We will make our own trade deals and make our own laws. We'll get a great deal and we'll save a fortune in weekly EU contributions. We'll stop immigration and go back to the good old days.

If we take just those five potential advantages of Brexit we can easily summarize how for each of those individual areas Brexit will not deliver what the leading Leave campaigners stated during the referendum.

In terms of trade deals, yes we can make our own trade deals in the event of Brexit. However if we want to continue trading with our largest trading partner (the EU) then those additional deals will have to be tailored so they don't conflict with EU standards. In any case our International Trade Secretary hasn't been able to make the deals he once insisted would be ready in time for leaving. This is simply due to the fact that the UK as part of the EU is a much bigger player than Britain on its own could ever hope to be. Third Countries are aware of that fact and have been extremely tough negotiators as a result. What we then are left with is the choice between continuing to trade with our largest partner the EU and the rest of the world on current terms (remaining in the EU or a very soft Brexit). Or we trade with the EU on much less favourable terms and still struggle to make other trade deals to make up the shortfall (No deal or hard Brexit).

As regards laws and regulations, yes we could remove ourselves from the jurisdiction of the European Court of Justice and EU regulation. However that won't benefit consumers, workers or the vast majority of UK citizens since the majority of the laws and regulations we inherit from the EU are hugely beneficial to society as a whole. I for one don't want to allow a Tory government to roll back regulations and standards on food safety or hygiene, nor do I want them to remove the current legislation ensuring that employees receive paid holidays from full time employment.

In chapter five we outlined how the easiest deal in history became a mediocre deal and that mediocre deal is increasingly looking like no deal. I heard an analogy recently that all of this talk of the current withdrawal agreement versus a no deal Brexit was like arguing over the silver and bronze medals whilst pretending that the gold medal doesn't exist. As I mentioned in chapter three, at the minute we really have quite a good deal. If we were to leave and subsequently rejoin the EU then the terms would not be nearly as favourable.

In terms of our weekly EU contributions, we now know that figure was never the £350 million per week claimed by the Leave campaign. When we take the actual annual figure it's just over 30% of the total amount we pay annually in interest payments to service our national debt. A national debt that will quite literally balloon over the next few years, and take those interest payments with it in the event of no deal.

As regards immigration, recent figures have indicated that EU immigration into the UK hit a ten year low in 2018 so it seems the 'problem' was perhaps not as big an issue as the Leave campaign suggested. Perhaps we can prevent or limit immigration from the EU but if we do then that will be at the cost of British fruit rotting in the fields, literally. Along with farming many other industries will struggle to recruit. Immigration will continue from non EU countries as it does today and those who were so unhappy at having non UK nationals living and working in the UK might be disillusioned since EU citizens already in the UK are set to be given permanent leave to remain.

A no deal Brexit will result in an economic catastrophe, why would we want to self inflict such a wound on our economy and the wider social fabric of our society. What could we hope to change, in the end there will still be a government in place who will still take more of our money than we would care to give them by way of taxation. The main difference will be that we will all have less to give, and because we'll have less to give the government will need to take more to try to keep funding at current levels. Imagine austerity on steroids, the financial crisis in 2008 had global impact, the average worker however had little to no direct involvement in the events that led to that financial crisis. The only exception perhaps being that we all helped to fuel the crisis by buying houses at ever increasing prices. Purchasing houses for more than those houses were actually worth and thus helping to fuel the beast that was the subprime mortgage.

On this occasion if it's followed through to its conclusion, then the 17.4 million people who voted for Brexit, in effect will have voted for a self inflicted wound at least at some level. Not many of those 17.4 million people will ever have perceived a no deal Brexit since it was never mentioned as a possibility by the Leave campaign during the referendum. Yet the architects of Brexit are now claiming that's exactly what the people voted for. All previous talk from politicians saying that *"we will get the easiest deal in history"*, gradually changed to *"we are not preparing for no deal because there is going to be a deal"*. It has since become *"There is no problem with no deal, that's what people voted for"* despite every industry having highlighted the problems they would face in such a scenario.

Our politicians are literally ignoring common sense to push their own narrow agendas, because at the end of the day an MP on £77,379 per annum basic salary plus expenses and constituency costs isn't going to be on the breadline after Brexit. The same unfortunately cannot be said for the factory worker on minimum wage who now faces the very real prospect of losing their job due to their employer's inability to have frictionless trade within its supply chain. The single mother facing yet more benefit cuts due to Tory austerity won't do too well out of this either. In a few years when the country is practically bankrupt and taxes have gone up for the lower and middle class, those MPs will still be taking in their generous salaries and will sleep easy at night. Some may be in jail for the shameless lies that they told which would ultimately send the country down a path to ruin, but the majority will still be sitting comfortably in their nice houses with all of their home comforts. A no deal Brexit will certainly make the financial crisis of 2008 seem like a mere bump in the road. Every aspect of society and the economy would be impacted in some way yet the politicians seemingly don't care, if they go against their constituents they might lose that £77k basic salary and that really would be unthinkable.

You may have gathered by now that I'm a fan of analogies, I have one more that I hope will help to summarize my opinions on the Brexit Referendum, the vote to leave and the current shambles we find ourselves in regarding the potential for no deal.

In 2016 when the referendum was called the UK effectively had an ingrown toenail on our big toe (Brussels and the EU are that nail in case you hadn't gathered). With the referendum we had a decision to make, would we have surgery to repair or remove the ingrown toenail (I.e. the remain and reform the EU from within option) or would we instead choose to cut of our toe (I.e. the vote to leave). The UK decided to cut off it's big toe. Onward we went to enact article 50, at which point our big toe had been removed, we found it difficult to balance and walk (I.e. we couldn't effectively negotiate an acceptable exit deal). We ambled along on in that vein for for almost a year and a half, constantly tripping over ourselves as we tried to learn how walk again. We came up with a supposed plan with the chequers agreement followed by the withdrawal agreement. Effectively we would be cutting off our foot in order to solve the problem of an ingrown toenail, it was by no means perfect but at least we might be able to walk properly again with a prosthetic foot. Resignation after resignation followed and we started tripping over ourselves again, constantly trying to get up and change direction but to no avail, we just couldn't walk correctly without our big toe and nobody was willing to accept the withdrawal agreement we had made with the EU (i.e. removing our foot).

Along came far right Brexiteers in the Tory party with some potential solutions, much better solutions according to them. Rather than cutting off our foot as the prime minister would have us do, instead we should either fully pursue a hard Brexit by cutting off our entire leg or failing that we should cut off both legs with a no deal scenario, just in case the big toe on the other foot ever had any ideas about becoming ingrown in the future.

At this point in time we had no toe, we were struggling to walk properly but at least we still had both legs and our foot. Quite why nobody was willing to contemplate the possibility of having a rethink, changing our mind and getting a prosthetic toe (a second referendum or decision to revoke article 50 and remain in EU) remained a mystery.

Onwards we marched to the point we were getting close to the 29th of March 2019. Our options had now seemingly dwindled at this point, the option of having a prosthetic toe fitted (i.e. a second referendum or extending article 50) was taken off the table because we waited too long. The foot had become infected and gangrenous (the relationship with the EU had deteriorated to the point no deal was looking like the most likely outcome). In the days leading up to the 29th of March we were going to be left with only two choices, seemingly now we had to choose between cutting off our foot (the current withdrawal agreement) or having both our legs removed (the no deal scenario).

MPs failure to remove the possibility of a no deal scenario, seemingly winding down the clock for the sole purpose of keeping the Tory party together and forcing a decision on parliament in the days leading up to the 29th of March is the situation we now find ourselves in. It may transpire that decision is delayed until June but at that point Parliament will again be faced with the same dilemma. We may be left with the binary decision to cut off our foot with the current withdrawal agreement or cut off both legs as the ERG would seemingly prefer. If that's the case and we choose the latter, then history will not forgive those MPs who voted against the many amendments put before parliament in January and February 2019 to rule out the possibility of no deal indefinitely.

If it does come to a people's vote then is it really anti-democratic to see what the population as a whole wants to do now, given that two and a half years ago some people thought they were voting to give the NHS £350 million extra per week (which was never possible given the maths). Others thought we would still be allowed to have access to the single market whilst being allowed to make separate trade deals globally, we now know that will never be the case. The leave camp has changed its tune so much over the past two and a half years from "no deal is not an option as it would cause economic ruin", to it now becoming their favoured option. Demographics have changed. Did people really vote for factories to close, food prices to rise dramatically, food choices to be reduced in our supermarkets? The economy to slow down as people have less money in their pockets, the eventual inevitable increase in taxes to help to pay for all the additional people who will need to be on benefits to survive since their jobs will have gone etc. That really does not seem like a desirable outcome to me.

I'm not entirely sure myself that another referendum is the best option, nor am I 100% sure that, given the current situation remaining in the EU is the best option. I'm probably somewhere between 95% and 99% sure it's the best option. The 1% to 5% doubt I have in my mind is due to a number of factors. One reason I say that is because a second referendum, despite my own personal views would be deeply divisive. People who voted to leave would feel they had been ignored, whilst others would certainly be grateful for the chance to change their minds. It may give rise to increased activity from the far right, we've seen what that looks like in the United States with populism and the rise of Donald Trump. People who previously had little interest in Politics are now entrenched in their viewpoints on both the leave and the remain sides. A new Brexit party has formed and I dread to think how influential they could become if we were to remain in the EU, I doubt they could ever form a government but they could certainly take every opportunity to disrupt and sabotage any future government.

The vast majority of the people who are apparently now clamouring for a no deal Brexit or a hard Brexit have little idea what that will mean for the majority of us as we go about our day to day lives. I hope this book will have opened at least some peoples eyes as to what those outcomes would lead to. A no deal or hard Brexit will have a dramatic impact on the average working person in the UK. It will result in reduced wage growth across the board, job losses for some and increased taxes for the rest of us. Less choice in our supermarkets, a huge increase in inflation will lead to significantly more expensive products across every sector, at a time when almost everyone in the country will have less disposable income, the exception being the super rich. We will see a new wave of austerity to dwarf the austerity inflicted upon us by the Tory government since 2010. This in turn will lead to increased waiting lists in our NHS and reduced access to lifesaving drugs and surgery. Education budgets continuing to take a pummelling, cuts to defence budgets, policing and every other public sector across the board. We may see a reduction in immigration, but that will be at the cost of many industries and sectors which will subsequently struggle to recruit. A massive devaluation in sterling will exacerbate the impact of inflation, making products ever more expensive. We'll see more expensive holidays abroad for those who can afford them.

The single scariest outcome for me however, with a young family living in Northern Ireland is the impact that any return of a hard border will have on peace on this island. I do not want to have to bring my child up to witness the re-emergence of the conflict that we all hoped had been consigned to the past. I just hope that those in Westminster with the ability to prevent such a course of events are listening. My fear is that they are not.

AFTERWORD

If you have taken the time to read this book then I genuinely thank you. I wrote this to try to help inform as many people as possible of the potential dangers of a very aggressive hard Brexit or no deal. The reason I felt it was important to do so is because I'm genuinely worried for the future of this country. Having witnessed the nation become polarised over the past few years, it's easy to see how angry Remainers get at the prospect of a hard Brexit staring us in the face. Equally it's clear to see how angry Brexiteers get when any prospect of a second referendum, or the possibility of remaining is raised as a potential option.

Yes I'm aware that collectively we voted to leave in 2016. I'm aware that any second vote is not ideal in terms of democracy. I'd argue however that the misinformation peddled during the first referendum renders that point less meaningful. People are generally more informed now that they were in 2016 yet the vast majority are still unaware of the risks we face as we stare off the edge of a cliff. If this book has helped to open the eyes of even a small number of people to those risks then it will have served its purpose.

Again thank you for taking the time to read this. I'd ask you to help pass the messages in this book on to anyone and everyone that you can to help us to collectively make a difference. If you've enjoyed the book then please take two minutes to leave a review and share to try to pass this information as far and wide as possible.

www.ingramcontent.com/pod-product-compliance
Lightning Source LLC
Chambersburg PA
CBHW030656220526
45463CB00005B/1795